Dimes on the Sidewalk

Robyn S. Lane

robo
PUBLICATION

Dimes on the Sidewalk
By Robyn S. Lane
Robo Publication

Published by Robo Publication

Disclaimer:
This book is a memoir. I have tried to recreate events, locales and conversations from my memories of them. While this story is based on actual events, some names, places and conversations have been changed for dramatic purposes and to protect the identity of certain parties. Certain characters may be composites, or entirely fictitious. The views expressed in this memoir are solely mine and are in no way meant to disparage any of the persons included in the book.

Editor: Rebecca McCarthy, www.TheWrittenCoach.com
Cover design and book production: Nancy Ratkiewich, www.njrproductions.com

Library of Congress Control Number 2019920253

Publisher's Cataloging-In-Publication Data
(Prepared by The Donohue Group, Inc.)

Names: Lane, Robyn S, 1954- author.
Title: Dimes on the sidewalk / Robyn S. Lane.
Description: [Mount Kisco, New York] : Robo Publication, [2020]
Identifiers: ISBN 9781734283808 (paperback) | ISBN 9781734283815 (mobi) | ISBN 9781734283822 (ePub)
Subjects: LCSH: Lane, Robyn S., 1954---Family. | Widows--Biography. | Husbands--Death--Psychological aspects. | Marriage--Psychological aspects. | Loss (Psychology) | Self-realization in women.
Classification: LCC HQ1058 .L36 2020 (print) | LCC HQ1058 (ebook) | DDC 306.883092 B--dc23

To Mark

Always and Forever

CONTENTS

CHAPTER ONE

Two Mallard Ducks

The brook outside my bedroom window is uncharacteristically calm this morning. Most days, the trickling of water across stones awakens me from the warm slumber of a cold suburban New York night, but today, the piercing silence awakens me. Knowing something is different, but not quite alert enough to understand, I peek through the shade and see two mallard ducks gliding in the stillness.

At first glance I think there's only one, but then I see him. He is dark in color—an earthy brown that is somewhat camouflaged by the surrounding bank of the brook. The other is distinctly the color of gray ice—proud, head held high, clearly visible. I watch them glide, side by side, in peaceful harmony.

"It really is a couple's world," I whisper to no one. It would have been odd enough to see one, but there are two. They don't appear to be strangers; they couldn't be, given their synchronization, their peaceful aura, and the grace in which each circles the other.

Facing widowhood at age fifty-eight has sharpened my awareness of the twos in the world. I know a couple when I see it. I'm also watching my mother face impending widowhood. Even though she's eighty-seven years old and been married for sixty-eight years, it's still not easy.

My gaze returns to the ducks. I am unsure if the earthy one would be my father or mother at this time. He is fading, camouflaged by illness, but still gliding proudly with head held high. She seems as strong as the ice-gray mallard, but internally camouflaged and faded.

And I? I am no longer a mallard duck gliding serenely on the water, but I carry the traits of both a camouflaged presence and the strength of gray ice. How many times do I feel like an imposter of my own self, hidden behind actions that don't betray my thoughts and spirit? Sitting in a book group watching myself laugh, contribute, appearing to be a whole person enjoying a conversation about someone else's story, when all I feel is the disconnected understanding that I am not the person they see. I have read the words, but I do not know what they said. I am alone, pretending to be part of a whole.

As two sides of a coin, how often am I also the strength of gray ice? How many times have I adjusted my body when greeting my daughters to confirm their perception that I am strong, confident, and able to go on? I answer their questions with a steely resolve and a steady gaze. How would they know that once I leave them, the gaze lowers and the ice melts?

It is only now that I finally understand that the qualities of being camouflaged and of being gray ice are possibly one and the same. I ask myself if this is true for my ducks. Do they represent two parts of a whole or are they merely themselves, one earthy and camouflaged and one steely and strong?

I find it ironic that as one of a pair dies, the other assumes the heartbeat of both. Even as I live alone, internally I'm part of a pair. To the world, it was us and now it is me. I am a disoriented mallard duck in the brook searching for my missing mate.

I watch the birth of my grandchildren, one by one bringing me joy and blessings, but I return home and wait for the intimate discussion that never happens. Who does he look like? How shall we celebrate? Didn't we do a good job with our girls? Remember when we never thought we would see the day? I miss being in that special and revered place of being "we." I often walk the streets of the city, bustling as all New Yorkers do to reach their destination. I walk with the crowd and my heart races because I am convinced that this is over, and we will reunite on the next street corner. It was all a temporary arrangement and we will be us again.

I avert my eyes from the brook. Its beauty both pleases and distresses me.

I want the mallards to stay in my brook and remind me of those precious moments when life is nothing more than gliding with the one you love, but it is time to pick up my grandson from school, I need to get the sauce they love on the stove, there is a book to be finished, and there are calls to be made.

CHAPTER TWO

Roses in Bloom

As principal of a suburban New York elementary school, it was my custom to write weekly letters to parents and faculty, hoping to provide a perspective or moment of inspiration. These notes were often half-page updates about the week's events, but sometimes they were longer essays reflecting my thoughts about a timely topic. I have always believed that these communications helped foster a sense that we were all part of one school family. Over the years, I must have written close to 500 notes of varying length and complexity. Little did I know how one particular Thanksgiving message would become more than a holiday message. Its words would echo in my life for years to come.

It was 2011 and the piece was called "Roses in Bloom." I vividly remember writing it in the same way I did all my messages. Sitting on the stool I claimed as mine at my kitchen island, cup of coffee beside me at 5:30 a.m. My husband was up and readying himself for work and I always took this time as my own. Every day: a cup of coffee, the news in the background (ABC with Lori Stokes), reading emails, planning my day, signing birthday cards or staring at nothing. On this particular day, however, I didn't feel my usual need to rush; I was cozy and content on my stool.

The day seemed especially sunny and the light filtered in the windows with unusual brilliance and strength. There wasn't a cloud to be seen, and I poured myself a second cup of the most aromatic coffee I could remember enjoying in a long time. Humming "Everything" by Michael Bublé, I might have broken into a dance had my coffee cup not been so full. I noticed Lucy, our resident Yorkie, who had come out of her bed in the corner to look at me, as if to say "Hey, look at you today!" She cocked her fuzzy head and wagged her tail as if to tell me that she too felt the joy of the day. In fact, our entire family was feeling the rare kind of happiness that happens when you experience something so magical that you actually feel elevated from from your usual world—the kind of feeling you just don't want to come down from. We had just enjoyed a weekend of celebration. Our younger daughter had married, and her choice of husband overwhelmed us with joy. As I wrote my holiday message for the year, I felt uplifted, almost buoyant, and the words flowed from my heart onto the paper with uncharacteristic ease and fluidity.

I knew my message that year would absolutely reflect our joy, but I also remembered that for our school, November was a somber and sad month. Just a few years prior, tragically, we lost a student with an undetected heart problem and a teacher from suicide—both on separate Thanksgiving weekends. Both unexpected, both piercing the bubble of innocence that often surrounds a school filled with five-to-eleven-year-olds.

Perhaps my personal joy on this particular Thanksgiving filtered the grief of Thanksgivings past. My message included the following:

> I hear people say that November is the month of malaise. It gets dark earlier, the impending winter bites into the mirth and freedom of summer. We begin to nest, cleaning our closets, pulling out boots, and cooking comfort foods like meat loaf, mac and cheese and mashed potatoes. As leaves fall, so do our spirits. This theory could be supported by gauging the number of phone calls I receive from parents whose children have decided that school isn't easy or from my candy bowl, which my teachers have emptied to help them navigate report cards, assessments, and just plain November malaise. Yet, I am saying no this year. No to the malaise. Why? Because I no longer believe that roses can't bloom in November. And I have proof.

As I return from my daughter's wedding weekend, it would be natural for me to be on a wonderful high. But I also carry with me the weight of knowing that, as a community, we have lost two important people in our lives at Quaker Ridge in November, the month of malaise, the month where nothing blooms. But then I looked outside the window of my office at the rose bush my then-fourth-grade teachers planted for me when I first came to QR. They said they would be planting one each year until I was surrounded by a bed of roses. As I felt the sadness of what we have lost, I saw the buds. The rose bush was in bloom, with many more buds preparing to open. When I went home and shared this with my husband, Mark, he took me to the front of our house and showed me our own rose bushes, also in bloom. As we approach Thanksgiving, I believe we all have a choice this year: we can fall into the malaise of November or look beyond the shorter days and colder weather to the roses that bloom in November. No one is untouched by sadness or difficulty in life, but if we look for the roses in bloom, I am confident that we will find them.

When I finished my writing, I did as I always do. I asked Mark to read it before he left that morning. In his usual affirming manner, after he read it he looked up, smiled, and said, "I love your writing as much as I love your cooking!" I knew he meant it, but not everyone would agree that my cooking was something to be loved! Was I to interpret that comment to mean that he loved my holiday message but not everyone else would? I felt my gaze narrow as I looked into his brown puppy eyes for a little interpretation. My affirmation came when he quickly added, "Would you mind if I use that theme for my message this year? Just the idea." I couldn't have been happier.

It was only a few months later that Mark was diagnosed with a rare cancer of the blood vessels and by July he was gone.

Thanksgiving 2012 found me sitting on the same kitchen stool, a cup of coffee beside me, 5:30 a.m., the news in the background (still Lori Stokes, ABC), another Thanksgiving message to write. How could so much be the same and even more be different? The chair cushion was no longer comfortable, my coffee sat untouched, cold and bitter from being the bottom of the brew. As I desperately thought of words to put on paper for yet another Thanksgiving message, all that echoed in my brain was the unrelenting tick of the clock. I pictured myself smashing it, but then I'd need the energy to clean up the damage. Not happening. Looking outside, I noted the gray dreariness of November; even the squirrels were hidden away. I was cold and numb. Sighing, I tightened the belt on my robe and looked again to the TV.

How could Lori Stokes still be on the news, year after year, same time slot, same smile? What caused her unrelenting cheerfulness during the usual November malaise? Why was I so annoyed at her when just one year ago I understood exactly how one could feel the joy during days of darkness? Oh yes, how could I forget that this was different because these were my days of darkness and they felt very different when they were my own?

"Focus!" I said to myself. Oh yes, the Thanksgiving message yet to be written. The blank computer screen seemed to taunt me. "Go ahead. I dare you to write it." Well, maybe I simply couldn't write a message this year. The person I cared most about wasn't there to read it. He wasn't there to taste my cooking either. If I didn't cook anymore, then, perhaps I didn't need to write. I smiled as his words from the year before resonated in my ear. "I love your writing as much as I love your cooking." I suddenly knew that there was something I had put off doing that I needed to do now.

I searched the inbox of my computer and there it was, unopened and threatening to destroy any vestige of strength I had gathered over the past few months. The video had been sent to me by Mark's closest colleague. His company created it to honor Mark's legacy and life. It was titled "Roses in Bloom: A Tribute to Mark L. Lane."

I was stunned. I do not know how long I sat perched on my stool, unable to set the video in motion. I stared and stared at the face I loved so well, and I cried as my newborn grandson, his namesake, did for his first weeks of life. I watched it again and again and again. The final tribute page ended with his voice saying, "No one is untouched by sadness or difficulty in life, but if we look for the roses in bloom, I am confident that we will find them." My words, his words, what did it matter? It occurred to me that the words I spoke one year earlier were then spoken by him and finally chosen by others as words that were fitting for his tribute. In a surreal state, I felt his hand take mine as I walked outside to the place he showed me our roses blooming only one year before. I knew I was alone, but I swear I felt his hand squeezing mine, as if he could bring me back to that happier time. No, today I saw the thorns, large and prickly. I touched them and the pinch drew a small drop of blood. Jolted back to reality, I shivered and went inside. I thought back to the mallard ducks gliding in my brook. I felt now as I did then. When one of a pair dies, the other assumes the heart-beat of both. So it must be with our words.

The seasons continued to change, and I find myself retired and wistful. My morning habits remain. I smile at his picture on my kitchen counter and share my coffee with him. I think about how he loved my writing and my cooking. I think about how much better the world is today because he was in it, how much better a person I am because he loved me. The cushion on my stool has softened a bit, and I am finally able to write again. I often watch that video, I think about the various connotations roses now bring to me, and I look for signs that the roses are still in bloom. Now, I need only to look at a beautiful wooden box, its top carved as a tree with birds on each of its many branches, given to me by my children when I retired. On it is written the words, "We will always be with you as you look for the roses in bloom." These roses have traveled a long way. With them, they have brought me hope and a belief that our darkest days will also reap some joy even if only in the memory of having smelled them for a short while. I find great comfort in knowing that the roses still bloom. They are in the smiles of my children, the laughter of my grandchildren, and in the knowledge that they understand the importance of looking for them no matter how dark the day.

CHAPTER THREE

Pete

We all have superstars in our lives, but mine is a man few know. I don't recall when I affirmed that his name is Pete—we only knew him as "the mean guy at the yard." If I were the ages of my grandchildren, I would call him the mean guy at the yard too. Unfortunately, many adults in our small town have also identified him in that way.

I first met Pete in the summer of 2015, when I was moving our family into our vacation home nestled in what is known as one of the two crown jewels of the Jersey Shore. There's Summer Lake and there's Twain's Cove. I was happy to join the Twain's Cove community, only one square mile in size, with charming houses leading to the vast Atlantic Ocean. What a perfect place! The sidewalks were lined with trees, pristine lawns, and even fire hydrants and street signs that were painted yearly. This was a place of retreat. No city muck, no noise, and no garbage.

The "no garbage" piece is where Pete comes in. Our move brought tons of empty cardboard boxes and assorted trash. The mountain of brown cardboard was climbing high, and I noted that mine was the only house in sight that boasted a structure of trash. How could it be that I was the only one in town with garbage? Where were the plastic cans and blue recycling bins? I asked when trash pick-up was scheduled.

"Oh, we can just take it to the yard," my dear friend, already a resident of Twain's Cove, replied.

The yard?

"What on earth is the yard?" I asked, happy to be rid of the trash, yet exhausted at the prospect of having to take anything anywhere at that point.

"There's a yard in town for trash and recycling. We have weekly pick-up, but everyone just goes over to the yard when they collect the garbage."

"You mean a dump? What's the difference between a dump and a yard? I didn't know I was moving near a dump!" I responded.

"Well, there is a difference because of this guy. I think his name is Pete. He's the resident curmudgeon who sorts the trash and recyclables at the yard. He has a lot of rules, though, so I'll go with you. He can be cranky. Never smiles."

I would have done anything to get rid of the trash at this point, so we loaded three cars and drove a few short blocks to the yard. There he was.

Pete—just as my friend had said. I watched as other residents deferred to his directives. Trash in that can, corrugated boxes here, plastic and bottles there, papers over there, and any questionables had to be sorted by Pete himself.

Look at him! I thought. A weathered man of about . . . 70? Maybe younger but that weathered look could add some years. Approximately 5'10" and thin-to-average build, baggy-blue jeans, and a white long sleeve polo shirt. Then there was the large cigar fixed on his lip and the wide-brimmed cowboy hat shielding him from the fierce summer sun. As we waited on line with our trash, I squinted through the windshield of the car and noted his tan, leathered skin. I guess his hat hadn't worked too well. I could see, even at this distance, that his eyes were crystal blue, similar to the sky or the ocean on a clear day. I studied the cigar dangling from his lower lip and wondered how anyone could grunt orders without that cigar moving even an inch.

I was in awe. All the townies waited for his approval before placing their trash in the acceptable receptacles. No one questioned Pete—no one really spoke to Pete—but it was clear that everyone respected him. He was the gatekeeper of the trash and that was, apparently, an important job in Twain's Cove, New Jersey.

As I stood watching, I wondered how Pete came to be the yard man. Was this a paid position in the town of Twain's Cove? Was he a retiree looking to volunteer his time for a worthy cause? Our turn came, so I opened the trunk and walked over to Pete.

"Hi!" I cheerfully stated. "I just moved to Brooklyn Boulevard and I'm sorry I have so much trash. I was told you are the man to see."

"Uh huh," was all I got in return, as his finger directed the bag I was holding to the large metal bins labeled "metal," "plastic," "corrugated cardboard," and "bottles and glass." I noted that the cigar still did not move and I withdrew to fill the bins, knowing his eyes were upon me. When done, I waved and said, "Have a good day. See you soon!"

I couldn't stop thinking about Pete. Nestled in my newly made bed with fresh linens and a feeling of newness around me, I wondered about him. As I drank my morning coffee on the front porch, as the chimes I placed in the tree tinkled, I thought about him. As I walked the three blocks to the beach, sniffing the salty air and scouting out my parcel of sand for my repose, I thought of him. Mostly, I thought, *this is crazy. Why am*

I spending so much time thinking about a grumpy guy who guards the garbage in a town no one has heard of?

All sorts of questions filled my head. *Where was Pete from? Did he always live here? Was it his childhood wish to be the gate-keeper of the trash? Why was this job important to him? What did he go home to? Did he have a family? What else did he do?*

The only answer my friend had for me was that he knew Pete had been there for as long as my friend had been in Twain's Cove, which was going on twenty years.

I found myself delivering trash to the yard on a daily basis. Pete was there each day with the same blue jeans, the same white long sleeve shirt, and a fresh cigar firmly planted in his mouth. I greeted him with the same hello each day and when I was lucky, I was able to get a small wave in return.

Although not quite sure of the reason why, I was determined to make him smile before summer's end. It might be that Mark always told me that I could make anything happen, or it may have simply been the thrill of seeing my family's faces when I claimed victory, but no matter. I just wanted to win this one. I made a bet with my friends. The winner would receive an ice cream cone from the best local homemade ice cream shop down the shore. (Native New Jerseyans believe the name of the state says itself. It is referred to as "Jersey," not "New Jersey," and they never go "to the shore," "to the beach," or "to the ocean." They go "down the shore.") The best ice cream down the shore was at Twain's Cove's local home-made custard stand. My family and friends took me up on my challenge that I would single-handedly win Pete over, but secretly I'm pretty sure they thought I had left my senses in one of the dumpsters in the yard.

In order to win Pete over, I needed to do some research. I thought of his physique, his leathery skin, and the whole package that clearly identified him as a town character. In order to know how to reach him, I needed to understand what made him tick. I began to notice his environment. Each time I approached the yard, I was reminded of the aquarium in which one of my friends kept her pet iguana. Her pet would slide around its habitat all day, approaching the various rocks and grassy mounds with an attitude that was a cross between independent arrogance and an inviting appeal to follow behind him. Apparently, these pets can be either dominant and aggressive, or calm and docile. Pete appeared calm and docile in spite of the power he wielded over the yard. He moved slowly, very quietly, and often just gestured his directives. One would have to approach him cautiously until it became apparent that he would not attack. Once that was established, he wordlessly welcomed you into his space, but the rules were always his.

Fans of iguanas often share that all the training and petting in the world will not change their pet's inherent nature. Their personalities vary as much as humans do and all you can hope for is a mild-mannered pet that will thrive in an orderly place. My new friend, Pete, was certainly thriving in a space in which he has created much order! Eyes on the side of their heads, iguanas have excellent vision and razor-sharp memories. This helps them feel safe and in control of their environment. To understand this, just try to sneak a glass bottle into the paper bin at the yard when you think Pete isn't watching. The pole he uses to compact the trash will come at you from nowhere, and he'll remember that you are one to be watched.

As I left the yard, I hoped I was giving Pete the time he needed to trust that I would respect his rules. Short trips, no small talk, keeping my distance. The day came, however, when I became restless and ventured a different approach. Holding a pizza box that lacked the usual oil stain that classified it as trash, I approached Pete and asked him if this was considered recyclable cardboard or trash.

"I don't want to break the rules, you know," I nervously giggled.

"Leave it here," Pete returned in a soft whisper.

Not sure if I had just destroyed weeks of effort or if I had entered a new stage in our relationship, I retreated with a simple "thank you."

The weeks passed. I responded to the teasing questions from family and friends about how I was doing regarding my Pete project with an offhanded, "You'll see. Coming along."

I decided to take a break. I wanted Pete to miss me. I continued my normal summer activities and followed the weekly trash pick-up schedule. No trips to the yard, no more talk of making grumpy garbage keepers smile. Off limits until the Fourth of July—three weeks away. I could not have predicted, however, what would happen in those three weeks.

I found myself having the extra time to walk the manicured sidewalks of Twain's Cove. Each house presented its unique charm. Front porches, some large with billowing cushions on wicker chairs, some boasting an inviting hammock in the corner, others lined with carefully tended flower pots. Each home was beachy in feel and personalized with its own shade of nautical blue, sunshine yellow or seaside gray. No two were alike, but they all worked together to create a tapestry of beauty. Here and there were what were known as "Twain's Covers," the charming but original summer homes that were waiting to be bought, knocked down, and rebuilt.

The boardwalk was unlike others I have known. Very quiet, very peaceful. Here there were no game arcades, food stands, loud music, or throngs of people milling about. To walk the "boards" in Twain's Cove was a Zen-like experience. Beach wagons held all the towels, toys, beach chairs, umbrellas, and tired children, and lined the perimeter, waiting for their families' return. Each block had its own entrance to the beach and fresh white paint on the pale gray planks of the boardwalk indicated which block it was. Twain's Cove's finest homes aligned the boardwalk path, each with its own special plankway from house to the Boards. Benches dotted the length of the one-mile span and a gazebo at each end of the Boards framed this peaceful picture.

The morning joggers smiled and said good morning, the silver citizens grouped together as they walked their daily two miles and the college students working as beach pass checkers at each entrance caught up on their summer reading as they looked up to acknowledge the familiar faces of beachgoers. There were no "shoobies" here, a south Jersey term for daytrippers who packed lunches in a shoe box and paid an entrance fee to stay. But a mere $10 would cover you if you left your lunch behind and bought one at the snack stand in the gazebo.

My greatest joy was to linger at the beach each day. I developed a particular fondness for the six o'clock dinner hour when the beach emptied itself of frolicking children, massive umbrellas, rainbows of towels, and the permeating scent of sun lotion. Not yet dusk, but shaded enough to sit in the naked sun, I noticed a new set of beach lovers. I thought of them as the dusk worshippers, and I found myself longing to belong to this group of beachcombers. They walked the ocean's edge with long-sleeved cover-ups to shield them from the shift in the wind. The breeze that came off the land in the day made the beach hot, but if you waited long enough for it to switch its direction and come off the ocean, you found yourself shivering and reaching for the closest towel. It was a magical time. All to be heard were the crashing waves, seagulls clamoring for dinner, the brisk wind and the sound of paws hitting the sand. This was the hour when dogs were allowed on the beach and their joy and sense of abandonment just made me smile.

Speaking of smiling, there he was! Pete! Was he smiling? I couldn't see, but the golden lab at his side certainly was. Still wearing his long-sleeve white polo shirt and wide-brimmed hat, he look like he had been transplanted from a penned-in yard filled with trash to a most magnificent stretch of beach whose only border was that of pristine sand. His profile was clear enough for me to see the extended cigar, but his gait was not the slow and deliberate one I had come to know so well. A stick in hand, he propelled it for his tail-wagging friend to fetch. The dog returned it to him over and over again, as if they had all the time in the world for games and frivolity. I watched him fade from view and remained in my spot until I saw his blurred figure come back into sight. He was patting his dog's head as they finally walked the sandy path off the beach.

As I watched this each evening, I felt tempted to interrupt, to say hi, to get that smile. But something felt very private about his time with his dog. Something felt like this would be a terrible intrusion and that my time to see Pete was back at the yard.

* * * * *

The Fourth of July typically involves all five grandchildren, my mother, and my adult children. The days fill up with bike rides along the boardwalk, the collection of seashells along the ocean's edge, roasted marshmallows while watching the blazing orange sunset, and the typical full-fledged barbecues. So much fun—so much trash!

The time had come, and I wanted witnesses. After all, how could I prove that I won the bet if no one was there to see it? Similar to the day we moved in, we loaded the car, and my friend and sons-in-law took off for the yard.

This time, Pete waved as he saw us enter. I stopped the car, popped the trunk, and got down to business. "Happy Fourth, Pete! I hope you had the day for yourself. It's so hot, isn't it?"

"Yup," was the answer that came back to me.

"You know, you have to teach me about some of this stuff," I stated with the confidence of knowing something I didn't understand before. "I'm never sure which bin things go in, and I need to get this right," I declared as all sets of eyes watched to catch Pete's smile.

Then it happened. Cigar in place, Pete smiled ever so slightly. It might have been my imagination, but did I detect a sparkle in those blue eyes?

"Ok, then," he whispered. "It's not so hard. Corrugated cardboard is recycled differently than your household cardboard.

That stuff can go with the newspapers. The bottles and plastics go together over here, and you can just put regular trash in those dumpsters over there. The tape from all these Amazon boxes needs to come off and go in the trash. There's a bin here for that kind of small trash."

"Thanks so much!" I declared. "Who would have known how precise a business this is. You'll have to help me until I get it right! Have a great day!"

I turned to get into the car and heard the words I had been waiting for.

"You too!" and as I turned to wave, there it was like a flag in my face: the smile. Not just any smile, but one that caused him to remove the cigar for that ever-so-small moment.

I won! I had my witnesses, and there was a big sloppy ice cream cone in my future.

I thought a lot about the man I saw at the yard and the man I saw at the beach. This man was not a grumpy, mean man who craved power over other people's trash and recyclables. This man was a modern-day superhero. A man who showed up day after day, year after year, to protect the environment of a town he obviously loved. And when his work was done, he journeyed down the shore to enjoy the beauty of the environment he helped to preserve. A man who understood that seemingly tedious days could reap larger rewards. A man who showed us that real superheroes are not larger than life—they are much smaller, much simpler in their deeds, more humble, and always there.

Pete made me realize that the world needs more people like him, more who understand the wisdom in protecting what we love, knowing it can all disappear if it's not nurtured and tended to, even if that requires a little dirt. I rejoiced at my "aha" moment when I realized that this was not about Pete being remote or unfriendly; it was about myself and others not understanding that we needed to take greater charge of preserving what we most value. Pete was silent because he did not need to tell us where the trash belonged; he needed to show us that we too needed to own the trash as much as we wanted to own the beauty of the beach. Not being responsible for one would surely impact the other.

* * * * *

Since that time, Pete and I have enjoyed a special relationship at the yard. He still doesn't say much, but there is always the wave, always a smile now, and he usually points out what I need to know about the recyclables. Recently, I noticed a friend who occasionally joins him, and they quietly speak among themselves. More often than not, Pete tells me to just leave my bags there and he will take care of them.

I no longer have the need to know everything about Pete. It matters not what he does, where he lives, what he has done on his journey. It matters that he is here now and is who I turn to when my grandsons need an example of a man living a purposeful, meaningful life on his own terms. I suspect that the story of Pete will be with my family for a long time. He may never know it, but this superhero will have a forever place in my heart.

CHAPTER FOUR

Grandma's Cookies

J was nine months pregnant with my first child, and it was one of the hottest Augusts on record. In 1980, doctors did not induce labor until you were two weeks past your due date. Well into my sixth day, I felt anxious, restless, and very big. Mark thought it would be a good idea to have my grandma visit for a few days.

"It will be a good distraction, and she can teach you some of her recipes," he claimed.

"Why not?" I agreed. After all, she was an amazing cook and I, at age twenty-seven, was most certainly lacking skill in that department. My husband was the only one who praised whatever meal I conjured up, but I figured I could use some help for my impending new role as a mother.

Poised on the threshold of being a parent filled me with excitement and fear. For each day I was overdue, I thought more and more about everything I didn't know, and the fear usually outweighed the excitement. How would I become the mother that my child would want to emulate years down the road? What was it that made a home cozy and safe for children, their safe place to fall?

I thought back to my own childhood. Music and food were definitely entrées into the world of comfort. Coming home from school to chocolate milk and freshly baked cookies, their rich aroma filling the air, was always going to be a good thing. Yes, Grandma was needed.

It was quickly arranged that Grandma would come over in two days and take me on a little cooking expedition right there in my own kitchen. Our first venture would be her famous cookies, composed of the perfect blend of cinnamon, nuts, and flaky dough. To eat one of these cookies was like having a magic spell placed on you. Friends and family begged for the recipe, but no one was successful in extracting it from my grandma. I, however, would be the fortunate one to ensure that these cookies survived for the next generation.

Now eight days overdue, I sat at the kitchen counter, armed with paper and pen, and watched as Grandma rolled the dough and added her magic ingredients. I wanted to capture this recipe and lock it in a safe place. My baby's childhood depended on it.

But things did not go as easily as planned. Like most expert bakers and chefs, my grandma did not measure her way through a recipe. In fact, there was no recipe. It was a "handful of this" and a "pinch of that."

"Grandma!" I pleaded. "Let me measure what you have in your hand. How much cinnamon did you just put in? Was that salt or sugar? How much?" She laughed and replied in her Yiddish accent, "A *bissel*, Robynu (she always added that "u" to the end of my name). A *bissel*." In case Yiddish isn't your native dialect, a *bissel* means "a little" or "a pinch" of something.

As a Jew from Romania who immigrated to America, my grandmother raised five daughters during the Great Depression of the 1920s. She did so by cooking and catering to the big hotels that were in their heyday in the famous Borscht Belt of the Catskill Mountains of upstate New York. Trucks would come to her Bronx apartment on a weekly basis to pick up her flaky kasha knishes, feathery potato and cheese pierogen, stuffed cabbage, and assortment of pastries. They didn't need to know her apartment number—they merely followed the melodies of smells that permeated the halls and doorways of the building. The mixture of cooked onions and savory spices combined with the scents of cinnamon, vanilla, and rising pastry dough led them directly to her door. I truly believe that my grandma single-handedly fed thousands of vacationers at the famous hotels such as Brown's, The Nevele, and Kutschers.

Not more than five feet tall, my grandma had snow white mounds of hair, slightly tinted by the blue rinse that women of that era added to keep their hair from the then-dreaded yellowish hue. I was always curious about this, as I had one grandmother whose hair was a dull white and this grandmother, whose hair was always snowy in appearance with just a touch of blue. I learned that this blue rinse, which is ironically still available but seldom used, neutralized the natural yellowing of white hair and was considered more appealing to women whose hair progressed from gray to white. Blue hair clearly outranked yellow hair in the days before all hair colors were considered acceptable.

Black orthopedic rubber sole shoes supported Grandma's tiny frame for hours upon hours of standing in place over a hot stove. When she wasn't standing in the kitchen, she was running around town in search of the freshest ingredients and the best prices.

Widowed when her five daughters were between five and fourteen years old, she was a hero in her own right. She tapped her greatest skill, taught herself how to read English, and began her catering business. During the summer months, she actually moved to one of the mountain hotels to meet the demands of the season. She was indeed used to hot kitchens, but that did not occur to me as we stood in my hot kitchen that August day. How could she look so cool, while I was drowning in sweat and fatigue? I may have been pregnant, but wasn't she *old?*

As I frantically tried to document her every move, my grandmother moved effortlessly around the kitchen. I wrote my estimations of the recipe ingredients on an index card and worried about how I would ever be able to replicate her art for my growing family. Why couldn't she just tell me how much she was using of each ingredient? I didn't want to admit it, but I was a little miffed.

I kept trying. "Grandma, where did you learn this recipe? Is it written down somewhere?"

She laughed. "I made it up, Robynu. When your mother was a little girl, she and her sisters were always in the kitchen looking for treats. I had big orders to fill, and I didn't have time for their fooling around. If I had a nickel, I gave it to them, and they went out to buy an ice cream sandwich. They had to share it five ways, that one sandwich. Those years didn't give us many treats. I didn't have a nickel one day, so I took some extra dough and put it on the table. I told them to make their own cookies. I gave them some of the dough and a *bissel* cinnamon, sugar, and salt. They crushed the nuts and made balls from the dough. They flattened the dough and used their hands to make shapes. We baked the cookies. Agh! They were terrible. Later, when I had time, I made them better and they became their favorites."

"But how did you make them better? What did you do?" I asked, thinking this would get me the information I needed. I should have known better.

"Robynu, in Romania we just did it. You'll see. You won't need to write it down."

Okay. I'm giving up now, I thought, *dropping my pen to the table. I won't be that mother. I'll buy cookies from the bakery for my children. Maybe, if I'm lucky, I'll master the art of the boxed cake mix. If I bury the box in the trash can, maybe my kids will think I have magical powers in the kitchen. This creating stuff from scratch just isn't for me—face it.*

But then when the dough was rolled and all the ingredients were added, my grandmother looked at me and said, "Robynu, you need to go back to the store. I forgot one important thing. It is very important."

With the most serious face she had shown me all day, she told me that I needed to buy the very smallest can of pine-apple juice I could find. It could not be mid-size, it must be the smallest version of itself and it must be pineapple, not apricot or apple. Without it, the cookies could not be baked.

"Aha!" I brightened. *The magic ingredient! There is hope for me after all!*

I hauled my Tubby the Tuba body off the kitchen stool. If she could stand there all day in the hot kitchen, then I could venture out into the heat one more time. I was an overripe watermelon on an expedition to find the perfect can of pineapple juice.

No longer allowed to drive, I faced the job of walking into town. It was a breezeless, still morning, 10 a.m., but the thermometer had already climbed well beyond 95 degrees. The local Foodtown seemed miles away, but I was on a mission, and luckily enough I returned home with the prize: two six-ounce cans of pineapple juice. (I bought an extra can for good measure.)

I searched my drawers for a can opener, eager to see how much of this magic ingredient would be mixed in the dough. You can imagine my surprise when my grandmother told me that we would not need to open the can.

"Robynu," she said. "Watch." As I stood there, my grandmother proceeded to use the bottom of the can as a cookie cutter! No magic injection of pineapple juice, no secret ingredient that I would be privy to, nothing. Just a cookie cutter!

My mouth hung open, not knowing whether to cry or scream.

I traveled to practically another planet to get a can that was a certain size for a cookie cutter. Couldn't we have used a glass or another can that was sitting in my kitchen cabinet? Didn't anyone remember that I was almost ten months pregnant?

As my shock wore off, I started to laugh. How complex human beings can be! I could not extract one measurement from my grandmother for the ingredients to her cookie recipe. There were no ounces, cups, or tablespoons—only a series of pinches, dollops, and sprinkles—but when it came to cutting out the cookies, there was only one size can that would do, and the contents of that size can had to be pineapple.

The cookies were delicious, and I gave birth to our daughter two days later. I finally did master the boxed cake mix theory and did not throw away the evidence. No one ever asked me why the shape of my cookies was always the same—a small circle, never hearts or flowers. A small pineapple can forever sits on my pantry shelf. I occasionally replace it when it is outdated, not that it matters. It is never opened, but always in service. It's the genie's magic lamp that carries my grand-mother's wisdom and love. No cookie can taste the same without it—of this I am sure.

And in case you are wondering, it took a few years, but I did attempt the "recipe." Grandma was no longer alive, but she was at my side as I rolled the dough and added a pinch of this and a fingerful of that. It was on that day that I shared the secret of the pineapple juice can with my daughter. I told her the story of how a tiny woman worked her way out of a difficult time in life by making sure all of her cooking and baking contained the only magical ingredient that mattered— her love. While the cookies were not quite as delectable as my grandmother's, I must say they were as magical to my daughter as my boxed variety was. And, thanks to my grand- mother, I understood why.

CHAPTER FIVE

Dimes on the Sidewalk

y husband, Mark, passed away in July 2012. He was sixty years old and I was fifty-eight. The week of his funeral and *Shiva* filled the house with purpose and noise. Food, flowers, and hundreds of visitors provided the intended distraction that supposedly helps those in mourning survive the initial shock of death. It wasn't until that week ended, when I was lying on my deck chair staring into the sky, that I felt the haunting realization that I would never hear his car pull into the driveway again. I thought about the call I used to get every evening as he got off at our exit and let me know he was only a few minutes away. I would hear the chirp: "Purchase Street!" and I could boil the water for pasta, ignite the grill, or get the salad made.

I became afraid of losing the sound of his voice in my head. I played the last message he left for me on my cell phone over and over again. The voice! The upstate New York twang would be forever gone, and I found this unbearable and unforgivable. Who would say, "So, kid, what was with your day?" No one.

I didn't know where to find comfort. The green duffle bag that held his clothes from the hospital lay in the same place I had dropped it on the day he died. I picked it up and threw it, unopened, into the trash. I opened his closet, where his obsessively neat clothes stared back at me. Racks of suits, organized by color and season and wearing plastic shoulder covers to ward off dust, lined the walls. Meticulously folded sweaters and shirts waited neatly on the shelves. His shiny polished shoes covered the floor. I thought I should clean out the closet, but instead I grabbed the sleeves of his suits and inhaled the remnants of his cologne. I sobbed as I realized that I could not get rid of any of this. I just kept sniffing any piece of clothing that smelled like him and then dropped to the floor to stare at how the soles of his shoes had worn.

Moving from the closet to his nightstand, I read and reread the little notes with his scrawls on them. Phone messages from work, reminders of things to do, a twenty-dollar bill, loose change, stays for the collars of his shirts, reading glasses, and an array of miscellanies allowed me to hold on, but not to let go.

One day, I was watching *The Today Show* and saw Eben Alexander, the author of a book called *Proof of Heaven: A Neurosurgeon's Journey into the Afterlife*. He told the story of his near-death experience and returning to describe how his experience forever changed him. I bought the book, and it became the first of about a hundred books I read with varying views on the afterlife. I also searched the writings of Jewish scholars and learned that the door was, in fact, open to the possibility that we are not gone forever, and because of this, I developed an insatiable and totally unrealistic urge to find Mark. I googled his name, hoping some magical entity would reveal where he was. As if there were white pages for the departed!

My search led me to the possibility that mediums were the way in to this mystical connection. I stayed up nights researching names of mediums who were considered credible, with the hope that someone else's story would resonate with me. I read and read and read, hoping each story would bring me closer to finding Mark in another form. I didn't care what form that might be; I just wanted affirmation that he was still with me.

I began to select and talk to various mediums. I bought even more books and longingly watched episodes of Theresa Caputo's TV series, *Long Island Medium*. She could pick a person out in a crowd and tell them that she had a message for them from someone they had lost. People would come to her for a reading and would leave convinced that she had brought their loved one home to them. She told them to look for little signs, like dimes on a sidewalk, to know they were not alone.

Whatever was happening for all these people was not happening for me, but I still watched with interest and hope, and kept my eyes out for dimes everywhere.

"You know," I told my daughters, "the craziest thing happened. I was setting the table for Passover and for some reason I looked up and saw this black-and-white bird holding on to the side of the deck umbrella. It wasn't perched, it was sort of hanging there and it didn't move for the longest time. We don't have black-and-white birds around here. What do you think?

"You know what they say about ladybugs? Well, yesterday I saw one on my bathroom counter. It had six dots on each wing, and it never flew away. I could swear it was looking at me."

I ignored the sympathetic look in my daughters' eyes when they flatly responded, "Hmmm."

The mediums I spoke to were well-acclaimed, kind, and sounded very knowledgeable. They gave me bits and pieces of hope. They cautioned me that I could find what I was looking for if I allowed myself to feel my grief and be open to all possibilities. How could I feel my grief any more than I already did? Open to what possibilities? To the one that Mark might be sitting at the dinner table one night when I walked in the door? Not likely!

I knew I was gravitating toward a dark side of life. Each morning, I carefully applied cover-up to the rings I noticed under my eyes, blush to my cheeks that were pale and dull. My clothes were loose from the fifteen pounds I had lost, and it became so easy to just pull a black and dreary outfit from the closet each day.

But friends and family were vigilant. I was carefully watched. People started to notice the circles under my eyes, so I started taking Ambien to help me sleep. I became anxious when I found that it didn't help, so I increased the dose. But it still didn't work, so each night I would wait for the train to come down the track of my brain at lightning speed.

On and on it chugged, night after night, until I couldn't take it anymore. One night, after lying awake for hours, I picked up the journal of medical information I had kept through Mark's illness and read it. Each note was dated, so I could relive what we were doing six months, a year, two years, three years ago on the day and date. I read and reread this journal every night.

Since the Ambien wasn't working, I had to drink more coffee in the morning to jolt my brain awake. But then people noticed I was jittery, so I turned to Xanax to calm my nerves.

I was uncomfortable being watched, so I started to dress better, groom my hair, plant a smile on my face, and convince everyone that "I was doing better." It was a relief when my public backed off because "she seems to be doing okay." (To this day, I can't understand how it's possible that I went on shopping excursions with friends, played with my grandchildren, laughed during movies, and participated in life in a way that looked so vibrant on the outside, while I felt so dead on the inside.)

Ambien, coffee, Xanax, Ambien, coffee, Xanax . . . I went on and on like this for more than a year, until my prescriptions ran out. I thought of my son-in-law, who gave me an occasional Ambien that he carried for his cross-country work trips . . . but I wasn't going to start begging for drugs from my kids! At least I hadn't hit *that* low yet! I began to feel scared at what I might become. In the deep recesses of my mind, I called out to myself to come back to life, but I had no idea how.

I vividly remember the one rainy day when I lay in bed listening to the sounds of the brook outside my bedroom window. I looked to the left of me, where Mark always slept. There was no indentation of his head on the pillow and never would be. I could find all the black-and-white birds and all the ladybugs in the world, but none would be Mark in disguise. And so what if I found a dime on the sidewalk? It would still be just ten cents.

I climbed out of bed and took the prior night's reading materials in hand. I intentionally closed each dog-eared book, placed them in a tall pile, and carved a spot for them on my bookshelf. I picked up the package I had bought the day before and filled the now-empty space on my nightstand with Elena Ferrante's four-book series, starting with *My Brilliant Friend,* a saga about childhood friends growing up in Naples, Italy. I decided that these four fat novels would keep me busy and immersed in someone else's world, because I was done looking for answers.

I went downstairs to make pancakes for the brood that would be arriving soon for Sunday breakfast. Was I feeling lighter as I stirred the batter? I actually looked forward to the commotion of five grandchildren under the age of five converging at my kitchen table. I couldn't remember the last time I genuinely had felt glad that company was coming over, but I did that day.

While stirring, I became distracted by a memory. It was a day about a year prior, when my daughter Tina and I had a rare moment for coffee. I shared my thoughts with her about trying to find Mark. She simply sighed, raised one eyebrow in a triangular formation, and said, "Hmmm." I felt a sensation of heat rising from my toes to the top of my head. I didn't realize it at the time, but in my new state of alertness and mental clarity, it dawned on me that that's exactly what Mark would have done. He used to raise his eyebrow at her when she misbehaved as a little girl.

I poured the batter onto the hot buttered skillet, and suddenly, another flashback hit. Erika and I were braving the diner with my fifteen-month-old grandson, Reid. He innocently ate apples in his high chair while we talked, and then suddenly he dropped one . . . and his right eyebrow arched perfectly up in a triangular formation, while the left remained still and even. In that moment of remembering, I made the connection that this, too, was Mark's eyebrow. Not only that, but I also realized that when Reid grinned, it was like staring at one of Mark's baby pictures. Exact same face!

As I flipped the pancakes and finished setting the table, I thought, *How could it have taken me fifteen months to notice this?*

As the days and weeks wore on, I returned to work and got on with my life, forging a new path by myself, but every once in a while, I'd get an astonishing surprise.

I once received a phone call from my son-in-law, Michael, and he said, "Robo—we have a little opportunity."

Maybe it was the sound of his voice, maybe it was the fact that it was a male voice, maybe it was the affectionate nickname he had for me, but my eyes welled with tears because it was Mark who coined that term in our family. He used to rename any problem we had as an "opportunity." I shuddered but continued with the phone call.

After hanging up, I flopped back onto the sofa and pressed my fingers over my eyes to breathe and calm down. I wondered,

How would Mark resolve this major "opportunity" I'm having of living without him? I struggled to hear his voice reaching out to me. I imagined him saying, "Robyn, we had a plan, but G-d didn't see it that way. What do you think I would want you to be doing? You know I would never want you to be alone, to be hurting. I want you to be the survivor you have always been."

Ah, that word, "opportunity." It lives on, and I still shiver a bit when one of my girls calls me to say, "We have a little opportunity we need your help with."

Erika, my youngest daughter, said to me once on the phone, "Mom, Dad was right. You are such a worry!"

I gasped. Suddenly in my mind's eye, I saw Mark's half smile while he shook his head and said, "You are such a worry."

Yes, *worry*—not *worrier*.

Mark always said I was an elegant and classy lady, but always falling over myself, dropping things and banging into walls and doors. I was such a worry.

I also noticed how Erika had picked up Mark's habit of checking on me. She started to call on a regular basis and say, "What are you eating for dinner?"

"Who are you going out with?

"You can't clean the deck all by yourself!"

"What are you up to?"

And now, "You are such a worry."

If it were anyone else, I'd bristle. But not at Erika. She is my little pal—my little pebble that I carry around in my pocket.

How did she know that? When did Mark say that to her?

"No, I'm not. You have nothing to worry about. I get around just fine, thank you very much," I fought back, to both of them perhaps.

I'm extremely close with my oldest grandson, Ethan—the only one Mark knew. He often talked of Papa and asked questions about what he liked and what he did. I told him that Papa would have thought that at seven years old, Ethan would be old enough to have a little job around the beach house.

"I'll clean up at the pool, Grams," he said once he turned seven, "but what job can I do to be with you? Do you want to have a job together?"

When he said these words, it was like a lightning bolt hit my brain. Mark was six when he lost his Mimi, the person he was closest to, and he used to do anything to be with her. Mark told me how he once carried a big tub of laundry down the stairs without being asked, just to help his Mimi.

Ethan wants to help me all the time, but it wasn't until this conversation that I made the connection.

And then there is Matthew. Born six weeks after Mark died, a tintype of him in ways too big to ignore. It's almost as if Mark's fading breaths breathed life into the little boy waiting to be born. The large brown puppy eyes, the expression on his face when he's thinking, the hairline and blackish hair, the ear-to-ear smile and oh, the heart! Big, big heart and big, big determination. A compact little guy, shorter than his peers, with ears poking out from his adorable face in a way that just makes you want to smile. Everyone thinks it's uncanny and almost spooky how much he looks like Mark, but I think it's magical. I put his picture next to one of Mark's childhood pictures once and gasped. It also seems that as each day goes by, Matthew is growing to fill Mark's shoes—maybe not large in size but certainly grand in stature.

I remember one summer, stepping outside the back door of the beach house, Matthew asked me where I kept my rags. It was a curious question from a four-year-old. I thought maybe he needed some props for a pirate game, or he secretly needed to clean up a mess no one had yet discovered. When I asked him why he needed rags, he sheepishly smiled and said, "I haveta do something."

I later discovered him in the driveway, a bucket of water, hose, and those rags on the ground. Our big SUV towered over his slight body as he vigorously rubbed the bumper over and over again until it gleamed in the sun. Matthew worked his way around the car, little by little and piece by piece—a squirt with the hose, a dip in the bucket and a vigorous rub. My eyes glistened with tears as I felt the familiar ache kick in. Mark would have loved this more than anyone!

Known as our resident car nut, Mark started his car-cleaning rituals at the same age as Matthew by polishing his toy car in the driveway of his family home back in the 50s. No one had taught this to Matthew. No one told him that a hand-washed car was one of the best things in life. He simply knew, as Mark did, and he figured out a way to do it.

Matthew looked up and grinned at me. My heart jumped as I recognized the gleam in his eye and his subtle nod that signaled to me that Mark was here. Over time I grew to believe that Mark had chosen Matthew to carry his spirit.

The message was delivered late one summer afternoon at the beach. I buckled Matthew into his car seat so we could go out for ice cream, and then walked around to the driver's seat. As I slid into my seat and fumbled for the keys, I heard his little voice ask, "Grams, do you live alone?"

Jolted by the question, and the fact that my four-year-old Matthew was asking it, I leaned slightly on the steering wheel. The sun beat strongly on my head as I tried to find the right words for what seemed like an eternity. I looked back over the seat to see Matthew's big eyes looking inquisitively at me.

"Do you?" he repeated.

Worried that I could blow this, I slowly responded. "Well, yes, I do, Matthew, but Mommy and Auntie E lived with me and Papa before they grew up and had their own homes. But we are all still family. We just don't all live together anymore."

A bit of silence and then, "But Papa moved out when he died? And now you're alone?"

Do I skirt the death issue or hit it head on? Hmmm . . .

"Weeelll, I can never be alone as long as I love people in my life, and they love me. Matthew, I'm okay being alone in my house. You don't have to worry about that."

Silence again.

I looked back at him as he stared out the window. Slowly, he turned his head, and I noticed a new expression wash over his face. It was still Matthew, but there was a seriousness not often associated with him. He spoke with a voice much louder and clearer than usual. "When Papa comes home, you won't have to be alone anymore, Grams. You don't have to worry either."

And I won't. I finally understand that he's already here. He told me so.

CHAPTER SIX

A Step Below

oney, you can be whatever you want to be.

Words from a father to his daughter, circa 1968. I was the daughter and I knew, even at the age of fourteen, that I was the person my father believed in more than anyone in his life. I was raised with the belief that I could be an astronaut, a journalist, a world traveler, or a lawyer. I heard those words so often that I actually believed them.

In turn, I believed that my father could have been anything he wanted to be if given the right opportunities. He wrote beautiful poetry and songs—ones that I recite and sing to this very day—but fame didn't happen for him. He returned from the war to marry and support a family. For some reason, he chose me to carry his torch, and it wasn't long before that torch became mine.

In the mid-1960s, color TVs started selling in large numbers. Our black-and-white TV set of the 1950s and early 1960s was replaced by this marvel called color television. Our living room boasted a big TV console and the NBC evening news was suddenly a family affair, where we all gathered to watch the world "in living color."

My entire perspective on life changed as I was besieged with vivid, dramatic images on a nightly basis. I saw angry protestors, anti-establishment songs, drugged youth, and an overall dismal picture of American life. As the years passed, we watched the civil rights movement blend with the feminist movement, so that by the time I reached adolescence, all I could understand was that life was unfair and unequal for most people.

It was such a contrast from what I had seen on the black-and-white TV sitcoms and commercials in the late 50s and early 60s, where "all-American" families shared "all-American" family meals in their suburban houses with white picket fences. The contrast of the black-and-white images from the early 60s with the color images of the late 60s made it difficult for me to decipher which picture showed the real story of who we were. Were we the Beach Boys or the Grateful Dead?

This dichotomy played out in my own life. I was living in the Bronx in 1961 at the ripe old age of seven. We had a good gig in the Bronx. My grandparents lived in the building across the courtyard, and I spent much of my time there. We were a neighborhood where all the kids played together regardless of gender or age. In the summer months, we played until the light of day was gone. Stickball in the street, bicycle and tricycle races around the courtyard, jacks on the scratchy hard side-walk, hide and seek between the tall oak trees and scrubby bushes, until that one day when my mother called out the window for me to come in for supper . . .

I entered my building to find a man in a navy-blue jacket hovering near the elevator. Some sort of innate instinct told me to take the stairs, so I did, up the five flights with what I thought was him on my heels. I banged on our apartment door and looked behind me. Luckily, he was gone, but fear overtook my ability to clarify if he had followed me up those stairs or not. I remember hiding behind the flushometer in the bathroom until the police came to question me. We never found out who the man was, and the police never came back, but I realize today that this image was the perfect representation of the schizo-phrenia of the time. The simplicity of American life, of a child playing in the neighborhood, overshadowed by the national mood that something bad was happening.

The next thing I knew, we were moving out of the Bronx to the suburbs of Westchester County.

If one understood the messaging game being played at the time, then it was clear that Westchester was pulling for the America Is Great team. The suburbs were where the city dwellers moved to perpetuate the dream. Houses, grass lawns, brand-new Chevy Impalas, and metro north commutes to the city framed the landscape. The news that filled the TV screens of unrest and dissatisfaction seemed far away from the hills of Westchester. As long as the boys wore chinos and the girls wore knee-highs, we were safe.

But even the suburbs could not ignore the growing turbulence. Entering my teen years, I traded my knee-highs for bell-bottom jeans and believed I was supposed to be angry at something in order to save the world. If you weren't a groupie, you simply weren't. (The problem was that I was never a groupie at heart; I just wanted to fit in. I was becoming a teenager, after all!)

The messages I heard continued to confuse me, especially the one called feminism. I was obviously too young to have been involved in first-wave feminism in the early twentieth century, when women fought for political gain, i.e., the right to vote. This was second-wave feminism that I was seeing. It had evidently been at work since the end of World War II but was on the national stage now as a fight for workplace, sexuality, and reproductive rights. The confusion, however, was that this message was often tied in with the civil rights movement, the anti-Vietnam protests, and the fight for gay and lesbian rights. Feminism did not stand on its own platform and was even criticized as outdated and self-centered.

It was all very baffling to me. I heard the battle cry about unequal wages, lack of opportunity, and endless limitations placed upon women. The media pounded us day and night with slogans and rallies, and women refusing to wear bras. Betty Friedan, in her famous 1963 book, *The Feminine Mystique,* inspired many to declare:

> Each suburban wife struggles with it alone. As she made the beds, shopped for groceries, matched slipcover material, ate peanut butter sandwiches with her children, chauffeured Cub Scouts and Brownies, lay beside her husband at night, she was afraid to ask even of herself the silent question, "Is this all?"

Gloria Steinem followed her call to action in the late 60s and early 70s and offered new slogans to mark our path:

> Men should think twice before making widowhood women's only path to power.

My bafflement wasn't because I didn't understand. It wasn't because I didn't agree. It infuriated me. I was a woman, and I wanted equality. My confusion was because inequality wasn't the message I was hearing from the most important man in my life—my father.

Honey, you can be whatever you want to be.

Could my father be so advanced in his thinking that he simply understood what the feminists were saying? Wasn't I the lucky one to be able to go forth and show the world that I could make my own choices and have the strongest man I knew stand behind them?

Energized and feeling empowered in a world where others didn't seem to be, I took advantage of the confidence my father had placed in me. I managed to get myself into college a year early as part of an experimental program between my high school and Alfred University in upstate New York. I was on my way to becoming something great when I unexpectedly met the love of my life, Mark.

A boy from Syracuse, New York, with an upstate twang in his voice and the best smile I ever saw, stole my heart and propelled me toward making the first real life-altering decision of my life and so I defected from the dreams others had for me, and those I thought I had for myself, and married Mark smack in the middle of my college education.

Oops—can you hear the record scratching?

Honey, you can be whatever you want to be.

"But what I want to be is Mark's wife!"

I remember the bellowing voice. "You are NOT getting married."

"So, I can be whatever I want to be as long as it is something you approve of?" I screamed back.

"You're too young to know what you want. You had all these dreams, ideas for your life that you will never have if you get married."

"No, YOU had all these dreams for my life. Who says I can't have them if I am married? Just because you didn't . . . "

My father's face fell as he lamented the loss of his dreams for his daughter. No worldwide travels, no journalist in the family, no big-deal lawyer. He couldn't see how I could possibly have it all if I got married. It was at that moment that I realized that the man I thought was the first feminist in my life was really just my father not realizing that these were the very choices women did not want to make. They didn't want to pick between a person they loved and a career. They wanted both. That was the point. I thought he knew.

And so I made the best decision of my life. As much as I loved Mark when I married him, it was nothing compared to how much I loved him as we built our life together. Yes, I had gotten married at a time when women were screeching for independence, but I had kept my independence and still married the love of my life. The years would prove that no person in the world could champion my growth and success more than he could. No one wanted more for me than he did.

I put my education on hold while Mark attended graduate school. I worked for $90 a week as a bank teller and was ecstatic when I was promoted to a desk job for $110.

No one around me was happy, but Mark and I were. From a feminist point of view (although I believe there is a large range of thinking here), it might have seemed that I was submissive, that I gave up a lot to support a man. But they didn't know about the Wednesdays when I had to work late and I would drive up to see Mark sitting by the curb to save a parking spot for me, at the risk of a street fight. They didn't see that we would go upstairs to our apartment, where each Wednesday would mean lamb chops in the oven, my pjs and slippers on the bed, and the table set for my arrival home. Who was supporting whom?

I vividly remember my last day of work at the bank, when I went to my car to find Mark there. He picked me up and twirled me in the air, Mary Tyler Moore style, as he was infinitely happier than I was that I could now return to school and get back on that path. I even remember what I wore—my red spring coat (yes, we wore spring coats back then)—but the real significance is that I knew I had married a man who wanted more for me than he wanted for himself. Hadn't I hit the jackpot in being a woman who could have it all? I didn't need to be an astronaut, Daddy. I didn't need some THING to work. I needed my relationship to work and it did. I made this choice. Everyone said it was wrong, but it was mine to make and I've never had a day's regret.

There were times, however, when I wondered exactly what my gender was fighting for. In the 80s, I pursued my professional goals while raising two daughters. Women wanted the right to have equal opportunities in the workplace, but then once we did (sort of), we also went home to cook dinner, give baths, and clean the house. So, reality was having *two* full-time jobs instead of one. Mark was taking the early morning shift so I could begin my one-hour commute, but his career was growing in a demanding way. I still dealt with the daily household tasks and the basic scheduling of family life. My mind may not have been wasted, but it sure felt like mush!

There was one particular moment when it all came crashing down on me. I got home from work after a one-hour commute. Still dressed in my grey suit with a blouse that tied in a bow at the neckline (what was *that* all about?), with my big 80s hair and heels (picture Minnie Mouse on a bad day), I greeted my daughter and immediately went to the refrigerator to start defrosting and cleaning the freezer. There were no self-defrosting freezers back then (imagine that!) To make matters worse, when I opened the freezer door, I found the shaker of salt I had been looking for the night before. Record scratching again!

Honey, you can be anything you want to be.

Now, my dad was happy that I was building my career, but I was falling apart inside. It occurred to me that he was not such a feminist after all. He truly believed I could be anything I wanted to be, but he knew that it might not mean having it all. Choices would need to be made and mine had worried him greatly.

I did eventually get off that merry-go-round, pursued my graduate work in education, and lived happily ever after as a wife, mother, teacher, and elementary school principal. I never claimed it was an easy path, but I could claim that I was making my own choices, and I chose to have it all.

But here is what I want you, my reader friends, to know. I could never—repeat, never—have been able to accomplish any of this without my strongest supporter and advocate: Mark. He championed for me until the day he died. He was *my* feminist, as he was for his daughters. He didn't say it with words, he showed me with actions. *Mark* was the one who plopped the applications to law school in front of me. "You would make a great lawyer, you know." Mark was the one who called the ad in the paper to my attention. "Robyn, you always wanted to teach. This grad program is perfect for you. Why don't you give them a call?" Mark was the one who convened a family meeting when I got my first teaching job. Erika was going into first grade and Tina into third. "Girls, Mommy is going to start school when you do in September, and you and I are going to have to do more around here to help out."

I think back to the day when our divergent path took us to Albany, New York for four years. We wanted to join a synagogue and visited one of the popular ones in the community. The director took us on a tour and proudly announced that the congregation was so large that they had to perform two bar or bat mitzvahs at a time. That was fine, until he shared that the bar mitzvah (the boy) stood on a step above the bat mitzvah (the girl) during the service.

I didn't have to say a word. Mark looked at me, and we were out of there. I never had to say anything—he was our champion. No daughter of his was going to stand a step below anyone else, male or female, unless she wanted to, as I had done when I chose to become a bank teller while Mark finished graduate school, and as he had done when sitting on a curb saving parking spots for me.

That was the difference between my father and my husband. Mark would always understand that my daughters deserved the freedom to stay in or walk out. It would never be about the choice they made, but about their right to make it. He might not love the choice, but their choices would never be his losses. My dad might not have wanted me to stand a step below a boy and would have told me not to do it. Mark might not have liked it, but he understood that my ability to choose outweighed what the choice was. And in my thirty-nine years of marriage, I never felt anything but equal, and I was usually made to feel better than that.

I now have reached a reflective part of my life when I watch my two accomplished daughters make their way as wives, mothers, and professionals. I agree with the ongoing roar of the crowd when they say that not much has changed. I agree with that more today than I did when I was actually living it. I see the choices my daughters have to make and know these are as difficult now as they were then. What I partially disagree with, however, is the interpretation of what we have been fighting for. Like so many other women, I grew up in an age where there were more opportunities than there were for our mothers. However, there were too many opportunities we had to noisily claim as ours.

I wonder, however, if what lies hidden beneath the chants, even this many years later, is a deep desire every human being, male or female, feels to be championed by someone else, for someone else to want more for us than we even want for ourselves. Maybe it isn't the "what" that we really want as much as it is the connection we crave, so we can pursue a predictable path, or a path not usually taken without any uncertainty or doubt.

Yes, a woman should be able to do anything a man can do, but so should a man be able to have his freedom of choices.

This isn't about gender; this is about human beings supporting each other's dreams and aspirations whether they choose to build a life together or not.

Honey, you can be whatever you want to be.

What I wanted to be was a wife, mother, and professional. Mark made this all possible for me, and it led to my greatest fulfillment and happiness.

CHAPTER SEVEN

Knitting Needles

My mother is the most unbelievable knitter you ever saw. No, really. I'm not exaggerating. Yarn stores have begged her to work for them. She knits for everyone, and I've never discarded one of her works of art. One of her specialties is baby sweaters, but she doesn't work from a pattern. She invents the pattern as she goes along, with needles clicking faster than high heels running to meet a train. No two sweaters are the same, and each comes with a hat to match. Not only do my grandchildren have new creations from her, but they've also worn some of the sweaters their mothers wore as babies.

My mother's sweaters are perfect. You will not find a dropped stitch, a snag, or an uneven row of yarn. I've seen her complete a seemingly perfect sweater only to rip it apart and start again in a fury of discontent. I'm aghast when I see her do this but then think how in character it is for her. My mother appears as perfect as her sweaters. Not a hair out of place, not a wrinkle in her clothes, not an extra pound on her small frame, never in disarray or frazzled. She surrounds herself in the yarn of a story she has knit for herself for the world to see— no snags, no dropped stitches—just a beautiful self-made pattern of a perfectly presented life.

What must it be like to be trapped in a mind that requires such high standards? Is she a prisoner there, tangled in a web that does not allow for dropped stitches or snags? I can assure you her life was full of snags and almost always about dropped stitches and dreams. How does one cope when perceived realities are challenged on a daily basis?

I think back to Rhonda and Polly, the daughters of the doctor my mother worked for throughout my childhood. "Oh, Robyn. We wish she were *our* mother. You are so lucky." Little did they know that I was the one who witnessed my mother ripping the sweater of her life apart, over and over again, in order to create a more perfect one. They saw the beautiful creation, but I saw the rippled, frayed strands of destruction.

They weren't the ones standing in our apartment when my brother and I awoke on Sunday mornings taking bets on what would make my mother start yelling. Would it be my father suggesting a visit to see his brothers and our cousins? What about her sisters and their children? Why weren't we going to visit them? This was cause for my mother locking herself in our only bathroom for hours, until my brother or I would write a note in our brightest crayon begging her to come out. It might have been more that we had to pee than wanting her to come out, but it had the same effect.

They weren't the ones standing in our apartment when my mother hung out one of our fifth-floor windows, threatening to jump if we didn't do as she said.

They weren't the ones standing in our apartment when she locked my father out for a full week because he had to attend an overnight business meeting in New Jersey. (No, my father wasn't having an affair, readers; he was the most devoted unhappy husband around.) My brother and I took turns bringing him food we snuck out of the house to his car where he spent his nights. The chain was always on the door to the apartment, and he was found each evening begging to come in, only to be rejected as my brother and I pleaded to our mother to let him in. There was the eventual day when he returned, but not before I was told to stand between them so he could swear on my life that he would not do whatever grievous act he did again.

They weren't the ones standing in our apartment when she hit my brother's feet with wire hangers as he lay sleeping. Or when she broke my cherished chalkboard in half when I didn't clean out my closet to her satisfaction. Or when she made my father return the Barbie Dreamhouse I wanted so badly for my birthday because it took up too much room. My father was so happy to surprise me with it, and I am still unsure if I cried because I had to give up the Dreamhouse or because he actually returned it.

And, of course, they weren't in the room when my mother would storm out of the house and take the train to New York City, not to be heard from until late afternoon when she called. We all had to get on the phone and beg her to come home. Afterwards, we celebrated her homecoming with a family Chinese dinner.

Yes, my mother's sweaters are perfect and, in her mind, so are her memories of our life together. Re-scripted conversations, reconstructed relationships, reordered events, completely deleted incidents—sweaters unraveled and rebuilt to perfection.

I have not inherited her talent for knitting.

CHAPTER EIGHT

9 Clips

1. The Phone Call

How can someone answer the phone every time (yes, every time!) sounding like a death march? "I'm all right . . . how are you . . . "

That quiet, sad tone that begs me to pursue her, to make her tell me that she really isn't all right but is being brave for me.

Well, I won't do it.

With even greater than usual cheerfulness, I reply, "Good! I'm great. Just got home and getting ready for bed."

She proceeds to tell me why she isn't okay anyway.

"Quiet day. I didn't hear from anyone . . . *(long sigh)* . . . but it's okay . . ."

Really? Then why is she full of such good news: how sick my uncle is, how she spoke to her sisters and they are planning trips but she doesn't think she can go see them, how unhappy everyone at La Maison Assisted Living is, how there is nothing to do, how slow the service is in the dining room, how boring the food is, how nice a day it is but she wouldn't know because she didn't go out, how all the activities they offer are just not her cup of tea, how much she wants to see the kids and has been texting back and forth with them, how many messages there are on the freakin' answering machine that she doesn't understand?

That's a lot of news from someone who didn't hear from anyone today.

2. The Dinner

You think it's easy to take your anorexic mother to dinner? Here's a peek:

    Mom: What's good here?

      Me: Well, I've tried a bunch of things here, and they've all been good. You can get pizza, pasta, or a sandwich. What are you in the mood for?

    Mom: I'll have whatever you want.

Me:	You mean whatever I want you to have or whatever I am having?
Mom:	Whatever you're eating is fine.
Me:	I might have a burger.
Mom:	No, I couldn't eat that.
Me:	You don't have to eat what I eat. We have different tastes.
Mom:	But if you like it, I'll like it. Just order for me.
Me:	Then I should order you a burger?
Mom:	No, I told you I don't want a burger.
Me:	Then you don't want to eat what I am eating.
Mom:	What else is good here?

I eat my burger and fries. She ends up with a grilled chicken sandwich. The bun comes off, half of the chicken is cut into small pieces, a few fries are allowed, and the rest is boxed for tomorrow's dinner.

Mom:	I'm so full now. This will be plenty for tomorrow. Anything not to eat in that La Maison dining room. But you should eat the rest of my fries. They're good.

Thanks, but no thanks. I already feel like an elephant dining with a mouse.

3. The Salami Game

People don't serve salami anymore. Especially in the homes of Soul Cycle moms who never let a morsel of fat pass their lips. Gone are the days when we smeared a whole Hebrew National salami with duck sauce, popped it in the oven for an hour, chunked it, and served it up with toothpicks. My father would kill for that delectable moment. My mother decided long ago that salami would no longer be allowed in his diet. Probably a good idea, but once in a while . . .?

So, I was surprised when my daughter served it at a family gathering the other day. My mom stared at that salami for about ten minutes.

"Mom, do you want some?" I asked, "Sooo good."

"Oh, no! I never eat that. I'm just thinking how much your father would have loved that.

Yes, he would have loved it as much as he would have the other zillion times you told him no. At least now he didn't have to be teased by it. Although I would have surely snuck him a few bites on the side.

"Oh, how he loved a good salami."

Are we really going to continue this? Shut it down!

"Yes, he did." I stab a piece and put it in my mouth before walking away.

Boy, am I doubly happy I brought him that Hebrew National salami two weeks before he died. One of my best memories is seeing his face as he carved off a piece, closing his eyes as it passed his lips. Funny how what then seemed so naughty, now seems so right.

4. The Museum Trip

Life with my mother is often a game of cat and mouse. I make no apologies for the times I actually win!

I'm happy to see Cara, the activities director at La Maison, where my mother resides.

"Robyn, it's good to see you," she says. "Your mom is doing great!"

Really? That's not what I hear.

"Yes, she signed up for the museum trip," she tells me. "Look here. She said she would go if she didn't have a doctor's appointment."

Sure enough, it's her handwriting on the sign-up sheet for March 1.

"Cara, I'm so happy to see this. I didn't know."

That little sneak.

I know my mother, and I know she never forgets a date she has for a doctor's appointment.

March 11, huh? She knew. She has no intention of going! Smart little cookie! I am going to have to shift strategies. If she went, she would see that it's fun to get out and that she can do something without me.

I say nothing, but I call the doctor's office and reschedule this routine appointment for one of the many ailments she doesn't have. I wait to see if she mentions the trip. Nothing. But I get a lucky break when the transportation director stops me as I sign in for my visit.

"Can you bring this to your mother? She needs to sign this before going on the bus for the museum trip." *Can I? I'd be delighted!*

"Mom, I just saw Jenna. She was so excited to see your name on the sign-up for the museum. She needs you to sign the form for the bus. I didn't know you were going. That's great!"

"Oh no, I can't go. I looked on the calendar and I have a doctor's appointment. I told them I might. I was at dinner the other night and Angela signed me up."

Okay, I won't be totally evil and tell her I saw her handwriting and it was a few weeks ago. Just proceed immediately to the punch line.

"You know, I had to change the appointment and I'm sorry I forgot to tell you. I made it for the following week. I'm so glad it worked out and you can go!"

"Ooooh, okay. I guess that's good then."

I haven't seen her name on any sign-ups lately. Maybe I shot myself in the foot, but at least she got out once!

5. Thanksgiving at the Beach

We changed our Thanksgiving traditions after Mark passed away, and turkey day at the beach worked well. Two years ago, the plan was for a Wednesday-to-Sunday visit, but Erika and Michael would leave with their boys on Saturday to have a late Thanksgiving with Michael's family. My father was very excited about the trip, and my mother reluctantly agreed to skipping her sacred weekly hair appointment. All good. Until we got there . . .

"I didn't know Erika and Michael were leaving on Saturday! Maybe they can take us back with them so I can go to the beauty parlor."

"For chrissake, Barbara," said my dad, "Enough with the beauty parlor. Why can't you just let it be?"

"Well, Grandma, we would, but we are going directly to Michael's sister's house in New Jersey," explained Erika.

"Mom, I can get you an appointment here if you want," I offered.

"Oh, no! It's fine."

Thanksgiving Thursday arrived and with it came our cousins from Mark's side of the family. We were happy to be with them and have an additional piece of Mark with us that day.

Mid-meal, as we were helping ourselves to seconds at the kitchen island, cousin Ronald said, "Um, your mother just asked me if I would take her back with us tonight to New York." *She barely knows Ronald! Is she for real?*

"Ronald, no! You can't do that," I said, "They're in Westchester, and you're in the city. Thanksgiving night traffic? I am sooooo sorry. Forget it." *I'm gonna kill her.*

In hindsight, I probably shouldn't have, but I vented to Erika and Tina.

"Grandma, do you seriously want to go home tonight?" Erika asked. "Don't you want to be with Tina and the boys for the weekend?"

"What?!" chimed in Grandpa. "Who is going home tonight? For G-d's sake, Barbara. Don't you ever give up?"

"Okay, okay. I'm done. It's fine. I'll just use my knitting needle to scratch my head."

Maybe I should just call a car service. Sunday is a long way off.

6. Tina Gets a Taste of It

Mom: Tina, if you take me to the knitting store, we can pick out the yarn you like for Zoe's sweater.

Tina: Sure, Grandma. I know just what I want. I want lavender and white. I always said if I have a baby girl, I am going to dress her in lavender!

Arrival at the store finds Zoe asleep in the car seat.

Mom: You go in, Tina, and pick the exact yarn color you like, and I will go in after you to get the amount we need.

Tina: Okay. I won't be long because we have to get back to feed her and be home for the boys.

Five minutes later:

Tina: I found it! It's a perfect shade of lavender.

*Grandma goes in and the clock ticks on . . . and on . . .
and on . . .*

> Tina *(freaking out)*: Where is she? For G-d's sake! It's
> been almost thirty minutes. I can't go in and
> leave Zoe. Let me try her cell phone. No answer!

Dials the store number.

> Tina: Is there a little woman looking at baby
> yarn there?

> Store clerk: Yes, she is paying now.

Grandma comes back to the car.

> Tina *(yelling over Zoe's shrieks for food)*: Grandma,
> I gotta get home! Matthew will be home!

> Mom: Okay, but look at the yarn first.

> Tina: I can't look right now, but I know it's beautiful.
> Your sweaters are so special.

> Mom: What did you say? Why is Zoe crying?

> Tina: She needs to EAT!

*Tina pulls out of the lot and spots the yarn bag on the back
seat. Peeking out of the top is a bright fuchsia pink ball of yarn!*

> Tina: Grandma, I see pink. What happened to
> the lavender?

> Mom: Oh, this is much prettier. It's perfect for Zoe.

7. A Special Shopping Trip

Tina was getting married! Being our first daughter and my
parents' first granddaughter, everything she did created a
frenzy in our home. I did not yet have my dress, but my mother

couldn't relax until we got hers. So off to *The Elephant's Trunk,* Westchester's coveted dress-up store, we went.

Pause and understand: My mother is a size zero dripping wet. Her younger sister died from anorexia-related illnesses and the only thing between my mother and that was a daily toasted English muffin. Also understand that I am not a large person, but my appetite is intact; I never weigh myself, and I love ice cream. However, weight is a sensitive subject in my family.

Oh my G-d! I am in this dressing room alone with her and can't let her go out there. The arms! I think I am going to vomit.

She goes out anyway.

The family is silent. The saleswoman clasps her hands and with a big smile she turns to me and says, "Oh my! It must be so hard for you to have a mother like this. Isn't she beautiful?"

She's right about one thing. It is hard to have a mother like this. Doesn't she see the arms? And the neck? I may be tough sometimes, but I will not let my mother show up at Tina's wedding looking like a piece of spaghetti turned sideways.

"She always was the prettiest girl in the place!" my father beams.

This is insane!

"I think we should keep looking, Mom. We have so much time to decide."

I am NOT giving this woman the sale!

8. Just Say It!

"I just sit there and think about how much I miss him. I see and hear him around the apartment, and it gets so hard for me."

"I know, Mom. He is very missable. I miss him too."

Sobbing. Silence. Sobbing again.

Do I just level with her once and for all? Should I do it? We skirt around it all the time.

"Mom. You have every right to feel the way you do. To miss Dad and to feel like crying. I feel that I should say something comforting to you when you feel like that, but I need you to know why I am not very good at that."

"What are you saying? Of course I know. You lost your husband and now you lost your FATHER!"

Significant sobbing.

"Well, I am so sad about Dad—I loved him—but I knew that in the natural course of life I would someday lose him. As for Mark, I'm shaking my fist at G-d every day. It's just very difficult for me to comfort you, even though I do understand. So, don't think I am being callous, but I just can't stand the woe-is-me stories even if you have a right to tell them."

I said it! I did it to alleviate my guilt and to make it stop.

"I know. I know. You don't have to tell me. I'm your mother! I understand this."

Silence. New subject and all is well.

Later . . .

"Aaah, I don't know what to do. I lie awake all night and just stare. JUST STARE! Do you know what it's like to look across the bed and see no one there? I can't go near that side of the bed!"

Silence.

9. The Doctor's Visit

> Doctor: So, how have you been doing since the last time
> I saw you, Mrs. B.?

Mom: Well, let's just say I'm here. If it wasn't for my daughter I wouldn't be alive.

Jesus, really? Here we go.

Doctor: Really? Why do you say that?

Mom: Because it's true. I wouldn't have a reason to go on.

Doctor: Well, last time I prescribed something to help you feel a little better about your life. Have you been taking it?

This should be interesting. Of course not.

Mom: I took it for two days and it made me tired.

Doctor: Oh, well it couldn't have worked after only two days. It takes a few weeks to work. Tell me, are you sleeping?

Mom: Oh, no. I can't.

Doctor: So, why don't you try taking it at night and it could help you sleep, as well?

Ha! That's the voice of reason, but he doesn't know her. No way! But she'll give him her usual lip service.

Mom: I guess I could try.

Trust me, she won't.

Doctor: Yeah, try that. So, besides that, how have you been feeling?

Mom: Okay, I guess.

WHAT?! I have taken her to three doctors in the last month to rule out a heart attack, stroke, diverticulitis, cataracts, and a sinus condition. All checked out. Every doctor said the same thing: "You are the healthiest patient I will see today." I am actually much happier about that than she is. Is she going to tell him?!

> Doctor: Good. We should probably take some blood and schedule again in three months to see if you're feeling better from the medication.

I see it coming. Here it is . . .

> Mom: Blood work? I just had blood work done and it was fine.

> Doctor: You did? Who did you see for blood work? Was something wrong? Let me look on the computer. Hmmm . . . it looks like you've been seeing quite a few doctors. What was going on?

> Mom: Oh, my daughter wanted to reassure me because I was having a few issues.

Are you crazy? Yes, I wanted to reassure you and I also wanted to stop hearing the ailment of the day, not knowing if I should run to the emergency room or not!

Well, the visit must be over. He turns to me, as he always does at the end of our visit, and just so slightly rolls his eyes. *He understands!*

> Doctor: You have a choice to enjoy the rest of your life, Mrs. B. I hope you decide to do the things that bring you enjoyment.

I love this man.

CHAPTER NINE

The Horse Always Knows

It had been a long four years of living on a tightwire. I lived with outstretched arms, trying to stay balanced between a pillar of depression and despair at one end and a more distant pillar of comfort and happiness on the other. My days, and now years, were spent somewhere in the middle, always suspended between the two pillars.

In September 2016 my dear friend Maddie invited me to the Miraval Resort in Tucson, Arizona. Since our husbands' deaths, we had become great friends and incredibly compatible traveling buddies. We were restless for a trip that would soothe our bodies and awaken our souls. Arizona seemed manageable, but the real attraction was less in the resort and more in one special man at Miraval. His name was Wyatt Webb.

We didn't really know much about Wyatt. We had heard about him from Maddie's cousin, who visited the resort a few months back. She encouraged us to go, saying,

"I don't want to tell you too much, but Wyatt Webb is amazing. Make sure he'll be there when you go because you don't want to miss him. He'll have you work with horses, but . . . well I've already said too much. Just trust me—you won't believe the experience you'll have there!"

So we went.

As the founder of "The Equine Experience" at Miraval, Wyatt was a man with a horse and a whole lot more. At first glance, he looked like a throwback to the Wild West I knew in childhood. He wore a big old cowboy hat upon his bed of long white hair, framing his weathered face. With a beard and wire-rimmed glasses, he peered at us from the deepest, bluest eyes I have ever seen. The classic cowboy buckle gleamed from his belt, which held up a heavy pair of jeans. A big-pocketed vest held his trinkets atop a white, button-down shirt with sleeves rolled up to his elbows. Pointy saddle-colored boots with metal toes showed the dust of the day, and his worn-down heels showed that this was a man who had traveled far to be here.

At first glance, Wyatt appeared to be a man who didn't smile much. We saw him sitting at a round table with a newspaper spread in front of him, paying absolutely no attention to the group that formed a line around him, eager to meet him and hear what he had to say. He didn't say anything—not for a very long time. He sat there reading his paper. When he finally stood up, his height was imposing and his expression said, "Don't mess with me."

Maddie and I wondered if this was going to be for us. We felt far too nervous for a place that was supposed to bring us tranquility and peace of mind. But we were here and too curious to back out now. We came for the Equine Experience with Wyatt Webb and we certainly were going to live to talk about it.

True to the ranch experience, Wyatt corralled our group of nine into a hay-filled wagon without speaking a word. Two majestic horses pulled our load to a circular field enclosed by a split-rail fence. The horses stopped and Wyatt motioned us to sit on the benches beneath an overhang facing the fenced-in field. Looking around, I thought all nine of us looked grateful to be sitting in a shaded spot during the height of a 100-degree day in Arizona. Wyatt showed no sign of being hot as he perched himself on a stool facing us with no overhang to protect him.

He looked up and studied each of us carefully. He crossed his arms and leaned back on his stool with his feet planted firmly on the ground.

Clearing his throat, Wyatt spoke.

"My name is Wyatt and welcome to the Equine Experience. This is where horse sense meets common sense."

Okay, I thought, *this is getting interesting . . .*

"You're going to clean some hooves. Anyone think they'll have a problem doing that?" A pause. All nine of us shook our heads.

"Good. Anyone clean a horse's hoof before?"

Quiet again, with a concert of nine shaking heads.

"No problem. It isn't so hard."

The stern, weathered skin around his eyes softened and a big grin spread across his face as syrup spreads on a pancake. Those blue eyes glittered and gone was the man we thought we met. In his place was a milder, softer Wyatt.

"Now, before we get started, and I promise I will show you what to do, I want to talk about a few things. Every one of you is here for a different reason, but you all have the same thing in common. You all have been lied to. Think about what happens when a baby is born. Nothing but joy. If he's hungry, he gets fed. If he's dirty, he gets cleaned. When he's tired, he sleeps. When each need is met, he goes back into that state of joy. Babies don't know what it means to distrust or doubt. They don't know anything beyond their pure emotions based on basic needs. Then the adults get involved and change all that. We let them cry a bit more. We stop listening to 'em and decide for them if they're hungry or tired. They learn that the people they trust are inconsistent in how they behave toward them. Welcome to our scary world."

Wyatt proceeded to tell us his personal stories of failure and disillusionment. A native of rural Georgia, Wyatt spent over a decade as an entertainer in the music business, only to find himself addicted to drugs and alcohol. Ending up in Nashville at a rehab center, he began a long road of therapy. He ended up working at this center and eventually became a therapist and the head of an adolescent treatment center at the Sierra Tucson facility in Arizona. He has been employing his own brand of therapy for over twenty years and has been running the Equine Center at Miraval for a good part of that.

"Now, let's be clear," Wyatt continued. "I'm not here to change anyone's life or fill your heads with new ideas about therapy. But I was twenty-two years old when my counselor in Nashville saved my soul. Logan said this to me: 'If you want to achieve the peace, joy, and spiritual fulfillment that you want so badly, it depends on one thing and one thing only—your willingness simply to do something different.' So, you're gonna clean some hooves and the way you relate to this animal will tell us what you've learned in your life about how you relate to all living things. You'll understand this later, I promise. Oh, and one more thing. It's not about the horse."

Wyatt paused for what seemed an incredibly long time. He scanned the group and focused on each face one by one before he continued.

"You all have been conditioned to be externally focused on your relationships with others. How much time do you spend thinking about what others are thinking and feeling and coming up with stories about why people behave the way they do? But if I were to focus on you that way, I can't really connect with you because I am not being present with myself. I promise that today I will be present for you. I won't judge you, but I will observe. I will be here for you. You need to try to pay attention to what you're thinking and feeling.

"As you clean the hooves today, I am here for you if you ask me for help. I promise to tell you the truth and be kind, but I'll also be blunt. Shall we begin?"

Looking over at our group of nine, I felt relieved that I wasn't the only one who looked confused and a bit nervous. What could be so bad that he needed to "be here for us"? Was cleaning a horse's hooves that complicated?

"So, meet Moonlight," he said. "This ol' girl is as sweet as they come. She won't kick you or run away. She is here to let you clean her hooves." Wyatt took a lightweight metal pick from his pocket. He walked over to Moonlight and picked up her front left leg. He bent it to reach her hoof, cleaned the dirt from her hoof and put her leg back on the ground.

"Hold her leg firmly, squeeze the joint until she lifts her foot up to you. Clean the hoof and let go. That's what you do." Wyatt repeated the steps for us and asked who wanted to go first.

What I became aware of during that moment was how I had changed from the time we had entered the ring. I had been excited to come, eager to have a new experience and be with a horse. I realized that I had been sitting frozen in place as Wyatt spoke to us. I had unconsciously pulled my sunhat over my brow, pushing it farther down on my face to conceal myself from Wyatt's fixed stares. My mood had changed. Not sure why, I felt defensive, challenging, and even a little bit angry. I came to work with a horse—not to be told that every-thing I learned in my life was wrong.

"Who wants to go first?"

Wyatt's voice jolted me back to reality. *Oh no—not me!* I glanced at Maddie and saw her look down to avert a possible connection with Wyatt's piercing blue eyes. A moment of uncomfortable quiet until a thirty-something man stood up.

He was familiar. He was the guy Maddie and I had seen the night before in the dining room. He had been eating alone, and we wondered what brought a young guy like him to

Miraval. He looked like a computer geek sort of guy—on the tall side, lanky, and a bit shy looking. Thin, frameless glasses hung on his nose and his mouth was fixed in a permanent half grin. Seemed like a nice enough person, but I wondered what his demons were. We therapeutic spa groupies seemed to always be in search of something, whether it's comfort for our bodies or our troubled souls. It was our time out. A time we treasured to stop our world, sit still, and let someone touch our aching bodies and minds. It had been so long since caring and caressing hands touched me. So long since someone had also tried to soothe my aching brain and soul.

The computer geek approached Wyatt with the same half grin I had noticed the night before.

"What's your name?"

"Michael."

"So, Michael. Why are you here?"

"Well, I'm trying to sort some things out in my mind to help me make some decisions about my future."

"I see. What do you do?"

"I'm a gastroenterologist."

Whoa! You just never know!

"So, you are used to working with people's guts, right?"

A small laugh, "Yes, I guess so."

"So, tell me what your gut is telling you about what you're afraid of right now."

"I . . . don't think I'm afraid."

"Okay. You think you can go over there and clean Moonlight's hoof? Does anything about it make you nervous?"

"Well, I hope I can do it right."

"So, what would make that right or wrong? Look over there at all these people watching you. Do you think they are going to judge you?"

"No, I don't think so."

"So, stop worrying about that and go clean Moonlight's hoof." Wyatt handed Michael the pick and Michael approached Moonlight. He paused to look at the horse's face.

"What are you looking at her for?"

"Don't know," Michael mumbled.

"She doesn't want to be your friend. You don't have to connect with her."

Michael bent down and tried to lift Moonlight's leg. It was rigid and did not move. Michael shifted his body and tried again. Nothing. A third time with no success.

"Just lift her leg, bend the joint firmly, and clean the hoof. Try again," urged Wyatt. At that moment, Moonlight shifted her body and dumped a huge pile of dung about two feet from Michael's body. A wave of laughter filled the air from the group of nine. Michael looked at Wyatt.

"Why are you looking at me?" Wyatt questioned.

"Should I clean it up?"

"Should you? Do you want it to sit there all day?"

"No, but . . . "

"Would you like me to help you?"

"Yeah," Michael chuckled. "I really would."

"Then ask me."

"Would you help me clean it up?"

"It would be my pleasure," Wyatt said as he picked up a shovel and walked over to the pile of dung. As he shoveled it away and adjusted the dirt in its path, Wyatt addressed Michael and the group.

"We all tend to think we have to fix everything ourselves. That we are responsible for everything. Remember what Logan said: 'You need to be willing to do something different.' Ask for help!"

Wyatt refocused his attention on Michael, who was still standing beside Moonlight.

"Come over here for a second."

Michael maintained his half-grin as he left Moonlight and approached Wyatt.

"So, Dr. Gastroenterologist, where do you practice?

"Ohio. I work in a large hospital in Cleveland but am thinking about doing something smaller."

"Have you had a good career there?"

"Yes."

"Wow. You have important people in your life, Michael?"

"My parents."

"They must be very proud of you."

"I guess so."

"How many diplomas you got hanging on your office wall?"

" . . . None."

"You do have diplomas, right?"

"Yeah, but my parents have them in their house."

"I see. Why aren't they hanging on your walls? They were your accomplishments."

"Um, I never thought about it."

"So, you don't have your diplomas with you, and you are thinking of leaving where you are. Do you think you have been successful?"

"I guess so."

"Well, it sounds to me that you have been. Also sounds to me that you don't give yourself much credit. Do you feel like you want to go over there to Moonlight and be successful cleaning his hoof?"

"Yeah. I can try."

"Okay, but remember, it's never about the horse. Horses are sensitive creatures and they can tell who's next to 'em. She just wants you to be real."

Michael approached Moonlight, picked up her leg and poof! The leg bent and Michael was able to clean the hoof and put the leg down again. The group of nine clapped, but Michael's facial expression remained unchanged.

"Come over here," Wyatt gestured. "Do you never feel good when you accomplish something?"

"No, I feel good."

"Really? No smile. Nothing. You just did something you couldn't do before. So, you going to walk away from this and just let it sit in the pile of other accomplishments you've had without feeling good about any of them? Listen to me. When you go home, you get those diplomas out of your parents' house and mount them on your wall. I promise you that you will know what direction you want to go in once you realize what you're capable of doing. And for goodness sake, ask for some help!"

Michael returned to the group of nine. He smiled, but also wiped a tear from his cheek. My eyes filled, but I definitely didn't want to go next! I resumed my stance. Arms crossed, hat pushed low on my face, eyes down.

But I could feel Wyatt's gaze.

I peeked and saw him scanning the group. Maddie shifted uncomfortably next to me as Wyatt spoke. "Who's next? No takers? You. How about you?"

Whew, someone else's turn, I thought, and looked up.

(Gasp!)

Wyatt's baby blues were staring at me!

Oh G-d . . .

"Why don't you come up?"

I felt my feet move, but I wasn't sure I was all there. I approached Wyatt and stood still.

"What's your name and why are you here?" Being up close to Wyatt made me self-conscious. Those blue eyes were penetrating. I was sure he could read my mind, and I didn't know in that moment if I wanted to tell him the story of my whole life or clam up in resistance.

"Robyn. I'm here because I wanted to have a new experience and heard about the Equine Experience from some friends." Even as I said it, I didn't think he bought it.

"Hmmm. Okay. Where you from, Robyn?"

"New York."

"What are you afraid of?" His body shifted, and he crossed his arms. I noticed a slight bulge over his belt buckle, the sign of a man who relaxed at the end of a day with a good meal. His legs struck me as a bit bowed, but his stance was confident and strong.

"I'm not really afraid. Just a little nervous."

"Why are you nervous? Are you afraid of the horse?"

"No, not at all."

"You afraid of not being able to do it? Because I'm here to help you." He fixated his gaze on me and I knew he meant it.

"No, I just want to be able to do it."

"Do you always doubt yourself?"

"No." *Geez! What's with all the questions? Just give me the damn pick and I'll do it!*

As if he read my mind, Wyatt handed me the pick. "Then go do it. Here you go."

I took the pick from his hand and walked over to Moonlight. I stood near her head and looked in her eyes before gently patting her. I could smell the horse aroma--a mix between hay, carrots, and dirt. Her eyes were a milk chocolatey brown and to me they looked kind.

"Why in the hell did you do that?" blurted Wyatt. "You think if you make nice to her, she's gonna lift her hoof? Try it and let's see."

I took the stance Wyatt taught us to take and knelt down to lift Moonlight's leg. Stiff as a board. Without looking up, I shifted my weight and tried again. Nothing.

"Firmly place your thumb under her joint and squeeze," Wyatt coached.

I squeezed Moonlight's leg but to no avail.

"Squeeze it harder!" Wyatt yelled over to me. "I promise you that you can't hurt her. I wouldn't let that happen. Just squeeze the joint as hard as you can."

I rearranged my body once more and approached the leg. It felt so thin and fragile. I worried I would hurt her no matter what Wyatt said.

"Harder, I said." Wyatt was making me nervous.

The force of the midday sun was noticeable now, but I bore down with what I thought was an acceptable level of strength and squeezed Moonlight's joint. Still no luck.

I stood back up and looked over to Wyatt. He stood arms crossed with his hand on his chin. After what seemed like an eternal pause, he said, "So, do you always not believe what people say to you?"

My head jerked up in shock. What did he just say?

"I'm asking you. Do you not believe what people say to you? I promised you that you would not hurt her and yet you still didn't listen to me and get that joint to move. Who betrayed you? What's his name? Did he leave you hanging on to a promise he didn't keep?"

I looked up, not anticipating the sting of his words. "No," was all I could muster in response.

"Someone out there taught you that you can't believe what they say to you. You know who it is. Who broke your heart?"

I felt an energy take over my body that I couldn't identify. I began to tremble and blurted, "HE DIED!"

Wyatt nodded his head and said, "I am so sorry. Who died?"

"My husband."

"He promised he would always be with you and then he died. Can't think of a greater betrayal. I am so sorry. What was your husband's name?"

"Mark."

"I imagine you loved each other very much. I also imagine that you know he didn't want to betray you. But he did leave you and now you don't know what to believe is true in this world. Why in hell would you believe me when I tell you that squeezing the horse's joint hard won't hurt him? Come over here for a minute." Wyatt opened his arms to accept me in an embrace.

Tears rolling down my cheek, I sheepishly approached this man who magically changed from a rough rancher to a tender teddy bear.

"Look at me," he said. I turned my eyes up to meet his gaze. "I am truly sorry that you have felt so much pain and loss. But I want you to look at these people over here."

I turned to face the group of nine and looked for Maddie's face on the bench. I had forgotten they were there. I saw her with tissue in hand, quietly sobbing. Looking around, I saw that all the others were too. The sight made me cry out loud. The sound of my sobs was unrecognizable and came from a well deep inside me.

"Do you know all these people?"

"No, not really."

"Yet they are sitting there on that bench crying for you. Do you think they want you to feel this sad?"

"I wouldn't think so."

"What about Mark? Let's believe he is looking down on you this moment. What do you think he would want?"

Silence.

"Do you think he knows he is missed? Do you think he would want you to live in constant pain and doubt?"

"No."

"Wouldn't he want you to find some joy in life? You are carrying a heavy weight with you and it can be found in every relationship you have. You don't need to carry that anymore. Mark wants you to lose that great pain. You have permission to do it, I'm sure."

I looked at him in silence. I didn't understand how this had all happened. I didn't think this would happen.

"Here, take the pick again and go clean Moonlight's hoof."

I approached this beautiful animal that was standing so still waiting for me to take her leg. "Okay, Moonlight," I whispered.

I touched her leg and approached the joint. As if she knew how much I needed her, her leg immediately came up for me to clean the hoof.

I heard the clapping from the bench, and I heard Wyatt say, "You see, she knows you are being real now. She can trust you. Basically, horses can sense your conflicted feelings and get mixed messages about you. It's 'get real or get lost' with them."

Depleted, I returned to the bench. One by one, each person in the group encountered Moonlight. Most of it is a dim memory as my body still trembled and I didn't recognize the moment of lightness I felt. I snapped back when it became Maddie's turn and expected her experience to be much as mine.

"So, Maddie, why are you here and what are you afraid of?"

"Well, I am here with Robyn and I also lost my husband five years ago. I'm here to do something new and I'm afraid I won't be able to do it!"

"What do you do?"

"I own childcare centers in New York."

"So, you spend a lot of your life taking care of other people's needs?"

"Yeah, I guess so."

"So, do you know that you need to take care of your needs too?"

"It's harder."

"Yep, it can be. But you deserve to be cared for too. Why don't you go over there and see what Moonlight has to say about that?"

Maddie approached Moonlight, lifted her leg, squeezed the joint and cleaned the hoof on the first try! I started to clap.

She returned to Wyatt's side and he looked at her before saying, "I guess Moonlight knew you were real when you admitted that you need some care. Guess she showed you she cared for your need to clean her hoof. Good work."

Maddie slid onto the bench next to me and whispered, "I couldn't have done that if I didn't see you go up there first. I cried my eyes out when you were up there."

I was drained. We were done. Wyatt stood in front of the group. We all looked as limp as wet leaves as he asked us to remember a few things from the experience.

"Horses can help us look at everything we have learned from birth on. So, you just had the chance to speak the language of horses: energy. They reflect back to us what they feel from us. If you're blocked, they can't feel your energy and respond in same. When humans start to work with horses, things tend to not go so smoothly at first. Then humans make up reasons why. They diagnose the problem, and it usually is about the horse. Of course, you've seen that it isn't, but we keep on diagnosing problems in the same way we always have. But we can try something different—we can be willing to make a change. Instead of making it about the horse, try something new, and if it still doesn't work, ask for some help. I promise life will get easier just by doing that. Stop living in the world that's been created for you and start living in the one you create for yourself."

Back on the hay wagon, the group was quiet as we returned to the lodge. We each thanked Wyatt, said goodbye to each other, and walked back into our lives.

Maddie and I found a quiet spot and sat for a very long time. Neither one of us had the energy to debrief on the experience until much later that day.

One thing I will forever remember, however, is my gratefulness for Wyatt Webb and how for one afternoon I remembered what it felt like to be hopeful, to feel lighter, and to know that I was worth working for. I try every day.

I'm getting better at trusting others, but I still have much to learn. Wyatt asked if I often don't believe what others tell me. Before that day, I thought I did. But Wyatt was right in what he observed: Every time someone tells me not to worry, every time someone says that things will be all right or even tells me they will see me tomorrow, the voice in my head repeats what my heart has learned: *"Maybe, or maybe not . . . "*

CHAPTER TEN

Melvyn

The summer of 2017 marked the five-year anniversary of Mark's death. It had been especially difficult to accept the amount of time that passed. My life had become increasingly surrounded by new people and events that weren't there in 2012. I often pondered how Mark could have been here one day and gone the next and was also plagued by how things that didn't exist back then could become such an important part of my life now. New friends, grandchildren, homes, and experiences. Such was the cycle of life and death, I knew, but still it elicited a discomfort I found hard to explain. On a deep, unconscious level, I sought permanence—something to stay the same for a while, and not be susceptible to life's changes that jolted my soul like lightning strikes to a century-old tree.

So every couple of weeks, when I left New York to go to my beach house, I would take West Side Highway to the George

Washington Bridge, get on the NJ Turnpike to the Garden State Parkway, take Exit 98 to local toll roads, until eventually I would arrive at the one narrow bridge that brought me into Twain's Cove . . . and that's where I always saw Melvyn.

He stood with his fishing pole, and I would turn my head to catch his gaze. He'd grin broadly and offer a big wave back. Even though our moment of intimacy lasted for only a fraction of a second, its impact carried me all the way through the weekend, and when I left Twain's Cove by way of the overpass once again, his smile stayed with me throughout the trip home to New York.

I could cross that overpass at any time on any given day and he would be there. I didn't understand it. There was no access to this spot that connected two roads like thread in a needle. How was it possible to approach it by foot and then be perched like a bird on a limb, as if it was a natural place to be? His presence would have been easy to miss in the few seconds it took to cross that bridge, but to me he stood out like a sore thumb.

How does he even sit for so long on that railing? I used to wonder. It wasn't smooth like a split-rail fence, more like wooden spokes sticking up from a plank in uneven gaps of one or two feet. It seemed impossible to sit on such a landing and unthinkable to balance oneself for any length of time.

Yet, there he was. Fishing pole in one hand, a big wave with the other, and a supersized smile to send you on your way. *That's my Melvyn.*

Skin not quite ebony but beautifully dark, contrasted with the whiteness of his smile and eyes. Melvyn was broad in build and always adorned in a tan t-shirt and shorts. Most striking, however, was the gentleness he exuded to the world in the moments it took to pass him on that crossing. You knew, without hesitation, that he was not a crazy man sitting on an overpass all day fishing and waving to people. You could sense there was a purpose looming in his shadow—a reason for being in that spot every day.

I imagined exchanging greetings. In my mind I rolled down the window, waved, and said, "Hi, Mel! Good luck with the fish today," and he'd say, "Thanks, Robyn. Safe trip home!"

One weekend in July, I told my Twain's Cove friend about the joy I felt in seeing Mel whenever I crossed that bridge.

"You are one crazy lady," he laughed, but then he added, "did you notice that your Mel wasn't there the other day?" (This friend was actually the one who first pointed Mel's presence out to me a few years back.)

"No! I didn't go by yet," I responded. "Oh God, I hope he's okay . . . "

I grabbed my keys and thought about how long I had been tracking Mel. I first discovered him in 2012 when I was just a visitor in town. My focus on him increased after I bought the beach house in 2015. His presence became as reliable as the custard stand that withstood every seasonal storm to open up on Memorial Day weekend.

I drove to the overpass three times on the day my friend told me Mel was missing. He wasn't there. *Where could he be?* I wondered.

My mind churned over a few ideas and slipped into fantasy . . .

"Hey, Mel. I've gotten used to seeing you here every day. Where have you been?"

"Oh, wouldn't you like to know!" he said, pushing his khaki fishing hat up an inch with his index finger. "Truth is, I got a yearnin' for a sardine and mustard sandwich my Gramps and I used to eat back when he was teachin' me how to fish. Couldn't catch any sardines here, so I had to go get me some."

"Oh. Well I'm glad you're okay."

With Melvyn, I loved the predictability and assurance of knowing he was there. It brought out an obsessiveness in me that, at the time, I didn't quite understand. As I said, there is no place to pull over near the overpass, so all you can do is drive back and forth like some crazy stalker. With each drive by I found myself feeling an increased sense of panic, racing heart-beat, urgency, and *need*—I *had* to know where he was. Was he lying in a hospital somewhere as a John Doe? Did he pull up camp after so many years and just move on? Did his fish supply dry up? Did he suddenly lose faith in humanity because people stopped waving back to him?!

Days passed with no sight or sign of Melvyn, and I continued to imagine what my conversation with him might be . . .

"So, where did you go after you ate your sardine and mustard sandwich? Cause you didn't come back to the bridge."

"Well, I come and go."

"You should tell me when you aren't going to be there, you know. Then I won't spend my time looking for you."

"You don't need to waste your time, crazy lady. All I want to do is fish when I want and wave when I do."

At week's end, I returned to New York without my "Mel send-off." I explained the story to my mother, and she suggested we make plans to return and look for him. So just a few days later, I went back.

As our car approached the roadway into Twain's Cove, we both watched closely. The rain and fog of that day wasn't helping, and I knew I only had a split second to see if he was there or not. *Damn it!* The wipers oscillated furiously, and the rain was relentless. I couldn't see. My mother craned her neck to spot the man whose story had filled the car for the last two hours. She didn't see him.

At the house, after we unpacked a few groceries and settled on the porch, the gloomy day began to take hold. "Let's go back and look again," my mother said.

"Hmmm . . . maybe we should wait till the rain stops. Let's go later."

"Are you going to write about him?"

"I could, but I don't know anything about him. I only think I do. Maybe I should interview him. Oh my God, what if something happened to him and I never get the chance?"

The rain continued until early evening, when a crack of light pierced the looming clouds. My mother and I looked at each other and nodded. We were going back.

"He's there! He's there!" I screamed as we approached the viaduct.

"Where? I don't see anyone," replied my mother.

"I see the pole out there." The fog still hovered over the water and our eyes had to move quickly in the time it took to cross that bridge. A shadow of a figure sitting on the split-wood fence appeared and just as we crossed, a hand began to wave in the foggy mist.

"Stop," my mother declared. "You have to go talk to him."

"I have nowhere to put the car! But it's okay—now that I know he's there, I can come right back and talk to him next time I'm down here for the weekend. I just have to figure out how to get over there."

The rain resumed at a fierce pace. The next day, my mother and I tried to wait it out at the house, but eventually decided we would have to get moving if we were to make it back to New York before dark. When we reached the crossing on our return, the denseness of the air made it impossible to see the outline of a man or a fishing pole, so we just drove on.

"How did you come up with the name Melvyn?" asked my mother as we settled in for the long ride.

"Okay. Do you remember *Moby Dick* by Herman Melville? The main character, Ahab, was on a quest to kill Moby Dick, the killer whale, after he had lost a leg to another whale. Melville was a genius for using their relationship to mirror the human condition. Melville's last piece of writing, *Billy Budd*, was unfinished when he died and was left for others to interpret and complete. In all his pieces, Melville struggles with the complexity of mankind. I always thought it was fitting for him to leave the world with a question mark of what he intended for Billy Budd. It reminds me of my fishing man. One big question mark in a world of water, fish, and man, where his behavior is atypical and open to interpretation. I didn't want to name him Melville, so I came up with Melvyn, or Mel for short.

"Anyway, this Ahab character was relentless. All he wanted was revenge for the loss of his leg. The narrator of the book, Ishmael, went on this quest with him but provided the perspective of watching a crazy man's irrational attempt to find justice. I felt he was winking at his audience the whole time because he knew that even if Ahab got what he wanted, his leg would still be gone. Of course, Ahab was killed by Moby Dick—probably the only predictable part of the book."

I looked over to the passenger seat and the look on my mother's face said confusion. She didn't say the words, but I could hear them swirling around in her brain, *Maybe my daughter really is crazy . . .*

The following week, I made my usual trip to New Jersey. Alone this time for the two-hour haul, I thought about how I would be able to get near that overpass. *How did Mel get there? Did he live somewhere under that bridge?* Maybe it was a crazy idea to think I could get near him and safely return to write the story.

Please be there, please be there, I repeated to myself as I drove. *He has to be there. Of course he will be there. Why wouldn't he be there? He is always there except for a few times that I just missed him.*

As I approached Twain's Cove, I was glad to see that there was no rain, but the scorching sun was punishing. With the overpass just ahead of me, I squinted through the windshield and let up on the gas pedal. There were no cars behind me, so I had the perfect opportunity to really slow down and get a better look at the lay of the land. *This can't be . . .*

He wasn't there!

What was it he last said to me? ". . . I fish when I want and wave when I do. You don't need to waste your time, crazy lady." *He thinks he can come and go without any regard for my feelings?*

Argh! Why didn't I stop when I had the chance? I berated myself as I unpacked the car and entered the house. *Such a missed opportunity and now what? What if he never comes back?*

I was so invested in this story, like when you're reading a book and you never want it to end. You parcel out the number of pages you'll read at a clip just to preserve the experience, and then when the final page is turned, you feel like you lost a best friend. The characters fill your head for days until you are able to start a new book—a new story with the hope that it will fill you up as the last one did. That's how I felt. I had delayed introducing myself to Mel to keep the mystery of his story alive, but now the story might be lost to me forever!

"Hey, Mel," I asked him in my mind. "Did you ever read *Moby Dick?*"

"Saw the movie, but can't say I remember much 'cept an old guy with no leg looking for a whale. That the one?"

"Yeah, that's it. He was looking for Moby Dick to get revenge for losing his leg to a killer whale."

"That don't make much sense to me. He won't get his leg back by chasing another whale."

"Yeah, but he is driven to do it. Do you ever feel driven to sit here and fish?"

"Can't say I do. I just do what I do when I want to do it. Doesn't have to be much more than that."

"Oh, I think you got a reason for it somehow. I'd like to know."

"I'm not that guy in that book of yours. I'm just here because I'm here."

Unacceptable!

There was a whole summer in front of me and my mission was clear: Get Mel back into his reliable spot on the bridge.

My first plan was to change my daily routes. I decided to take the long way to the Farmers' Market each week, which would put me at Mel's lookout. I started getting gas at the station closest to Mel's post. I figured out all the ways I could cross Mel's path, and when I ran out of ideas, I would just go there.

I figured out that if I parked my car in the shopping plaza about a mile past the bridge, I could walk on the grass all the way back to it. Then if Mel was there, I could ask him how to get over to his spot. Maybe he would come down from the fence and come to me. *After all, he must like people if he waves to them all day long . . .*

I tried this approach the next morning with no luck.

I ventured out again mid-afternoon. No luck.

By late afternoon I was crazed enough to plant myself in the parking lot of that shopping strip. I waited for fifteen minutes and drove the mile to the bridge, then back to the lot to wait another fifteen minutes before trying again.

Looking around the lot during these intervals, I tried to see if any new cars appeared, perhaps driven by a man with a fishing pole. Maybe he had a car. Maybe he went into the diner and would be coming out to resume his post or go home.

As dusk approached, I rode over the bridge one more time on my way back to my beach house. No one was there.

Once more furious at myself for not stopping when I had the chance, I dropped into the rocker on my front porch and waited for my daily hummingbird visitors to come feast on the nectar I left in their feeder. I usually looked forward to this time of day. I knew they would come and go in fifteen-minute intervals, filling their bellies, preparing for their late summer migration.

Sure enough, they came. *(Phew!)*

"What am I going to do with myself?" I asked my bird friends out loud as they flittered around the feeder.

Suddenly, I felt one last surge of *Maybe now* . . . so I grabbed my car keys and headed to the bridge. *One more try* . . . Before pulling out of the driveway, I ran back in the house to grab my small journal. I was confident that I'd need it when I spoke to Mel.

Approaching the all-too-familiar crossing, I slowed the car. My heart skipped several beats as I saw the outline of a man sitting on the fence!

"I did it! I did it!" I shouted and pounded the steering wheel as my mind raced with plans to park the car and walk back to the overpass before it got too dark. With the sweet taste of victory in my mouth, I drove forward, only to slam on my brakes and stare in astonishment. This was not Melvyn! In his place was a younger, whiter, and less-friendly-looking person who was not smiling or waving to anyone.

What?!

In shock, I drove home.

As if to read my mood, the weather brought an uncharacteristic stretch of cool, rainy days. I spent many hours in my rocker, kicking sand, feeling morose, living in a cloud of purple and gray. Eventually I realized that, while my disappointment and confusion about Mel was strong, it wasn't nearly as powerful as the fear I developed for the way I was feeling—for my own sanity.

What's wrong with me? How could this stranger have such an impact on me? I wondered. I knew needed to snap out of it. I had a week before my kids and grandkids would be arriving for their final stay of the summer, so I decided to go back home to New York for a few days to regain some perspective. I crossed the bridge on my trip home and glanced to my right, unsure of what I wanted to see. There was nothing. No Mel, and no one else.

"Mel, where the hell have you been? Don't you know I count on you? Is this a responsible way to act when you know people are counting on you? You just can't disappear one day without any notice or reason."

"Watch me!" he smiled, then he snapped his fingers and vanished.

Don't do this, Robyn, I thought to myself over and over again. *This doesn't matter. Nothing happened here. It's in your head.*

Settling into bed that night, I found myself reaching for the bottle of Ambien I had long ago placed in my nightstand. I thought that maybe if I just got a good night's sleep, I would be able to forget about all that nonsense and feel better. I also heard the call of all the old books I had shelved—the ones with theories about where people go when they aren't here anymore.

"No," I said out loud. "I'm not going back to that dark place." As my tears soaked my pillow, I murmured, "I don't know who I am anymore."

At 4 a.m. I woke up suddenly, fully alert. I knew what I needed to do. I got up and went to sit in the chair by my window, looked at the moonlight skipping across the brook, and began . . .

"Hey, Mel. I'm sorry I got mad at you. You see, I was worried about you. I've been crossing this overpass day after day. I see you, I think I see you, and then I don't."

"Yeah, well, it gets like that sometimes. You can see things clearly one day and the next day it's all one big fog."

"Yeah, I suppose. Well, I came to say goodbye. I'll still be looking for you on that bridge, but I won't be bothering you anymore."

"Ok, Ahab. See you around."

Labor Day weekend brought the same noise and commotion to end the summer as Memorial Day had brought to start it just a few short months prior. I came downstairs Saturday morning to hear a conversation in progress between Ethan and Tina.

"Ethan, I'm not trying to be mean."

"Yes, you are! It's not fair. All I want to do is go down to the beach and come back."

"You can't go alone. Stop asking."

"You said I was old enough to do things by myself now, but then when I want to, you say no!"

"You can do things by yourself. But seven-year-olds don't go to the beach alone. It's just the way it is."

Hmmm . . . It's just the way it is.

Tina's words exploded in my head in a way I had never experienced before.

It's just the way it is.

The words left me feeling dizzy, like someone took the wind out of me through a punch to the stomach.

It's just the way it is, I repeated to myself over and over again. That's it. Some questions do not get answered, some truths are never revealed, and *it's just the way it is.*

The summer ended, and I witnessed the usual post-Labor Day exodus of Twain's Cove's summer residents. The beaches fell quiet, traffic disappeared, and restaurants no longer required reservations. Townies celebrated the arrival of September and called it their "autumn summer." Skies became clearer, the colors turned brighter, the sun hovered but didn't burn. It was a wonderful time of year, with no guests to entertain and no loads of laundry to wash, so I lingered a little before heading back to New York. After a few days of peace and quiet to air out, I left Twain's Cove for the final time until spring.

I settled in to the reliability of autumn with its falling leaves, shorter days, and yearnings for pumpkin spice and hot soup. I filled my calendar with routine doctor appointments and long-awaited dates with old friends. I learned that much was the same. The mallard ducks returned to the brook in my back yard. They knew the cool, clear water of autumn would be there for them. My grandchildren had their new back-to-school sneakers and backpacks lined up. My book group resumed.

One morning I took my regular trip to Starbucks for my hot skim Chai Tea Latte. I looked for Delia, who always knew my order and always got it ready as soon as she saw me approach the door. But that morning, Delia wasn't there.

I felt an urge stir within. It was familiar. It was the one that made me *need* to know where she went—the one that would make me mark her steps and trace her whereabouts. I felt it, but differently this time.

It's just the way it is.

I asked the new person at the counter, Sarah, where Delia was. She smiled, shrugged, and said, "I guess she just moved on to something else."

I smiled back and said, "Good for her. Can I have a skim Chai Tea Latte, please?"

CHAPTER ELEVEN

The Hum

The Hum is loud today. Normally suppressed and tucked away, it is wildly playing its tune to me (probably just to me, but that makes it even more special.)

At one end of the small narrow space stands Gabriel, owner of the shop. Neatly but comfortably dressed, he speaks softly to the forty-something woman whose hair he is trimming. The scraping of the scissors is muted as he carefully trims the ends of her hair with a delicate and swift motion.

Behind him, Bea, the sole shampooer of the shop, sweeps the fallen amber hair into a dustpan with soft and quick strokes. She is the sole shampooer less because of the size of the shop but more because she makes it impossible for anyone else to succeed there. To have your hair washed by Bea is synonymous with a visit to the spa. To be under her care is to have an impeccable wash followed by a ten-minute scalp massage that will either put you to sleep or transport you to another place for the duration of your visit. No matter how busy, no matter how many times Gabriel gives her the signal to move it along, Bea's allegiance is to the head in her chair, providing equal experiences to all who come.

Across from Gabriel and next to me stands Rubin. He's preparing himself for his next client, lining up his tools and checking his drawer for the weighted apron he places on his clients' necks to relax their shoulders. Tall and eager to engage in conversation, Rubin exudes an aura of happiness that he enthusiastically transmits to others around him.

In the concealed back area of the salon is Rosetta, the master of color. She stands with apron drawn around her body and gloves on her hands, preparing the magic potion that will transform some lucky person with graying roots into a high-lighted and glowing fairy princess. She hums a tune as she mixes the activator into the color with care and precision. Timing is important. No mixture is prepared prior to the client's arrival—she has to ensure the proper strength and consistency of the solution. Her robed and ready client patiently reads the latest bestseller while waiting for the application to begin.

The phone is uncharacteristically quiet, leaving Crystal, the front desk receptionist and office manager, to check appointments and survey the surrounding shelves for products that need replenishing or organization.

I usually find myself in Gabriel's chair, but today I'm sitting across from him in Roseanna's station. The truth is, I love the way Roseanna does my hair and don't mind that Gabriel is otherwise engaged. Gabriel has been my man for eight years and we share a mutual loyalty, but here is a place where I am content to have anyone in the shop work their magic on my thick, shoulder-length hair, often described as having a mind of its own.

I share my observations of these individuals because they're central to the Hum I hear today. They remind me of the Hum I can summon in moments such as these; the one that I never noticed until it was made infinitely loud by its absence.

From 1990 to 2002, I taught a multi-age class of fourth and fifth graders at West Patent Elementary School in Bedford, New York. I should correct myself—the actual Hum did not last all those years. The Hum lasted approximately four years, although it would be difficult to calculate an exact measure. It was an open-space multi-age school—the only one structured that way in a district of five elementary schools—unusual and, as we all believed, special. I entered the world of teaching this way. Mine was not an isolated and lonely experience as others have described the profession. Mine was one built on the thread of teamwork and companionship in an environment where there were no walls, no doors, and few borders to distinguish one stage of learning from another.

Our team was called Team IV and we had a reputation. Four strong women responsible for two years of education of ten- and eleven-year-olds before they were sent into the traditional halls of middle school. We felt we had to work extra hard to fight the ever-posed question: Do the West Patent kids do as well as everyone else? Are they as well-prepared for middle school as other kids? (Truth is, we didn't worry too much about the answer because we knew in our souls that they were more prepared for middle school than any of their peers from other schools could be. We focused much more on whether they were prepared for *life*. This may sound conceited to you, my readers, but we were not conceited. We were just proud.)

In addition to our team of four teachers, we had Ginger, the best teaching assistant in the school. Dina was our team secretary. (Yes, each team in the school had its own secretary!) You might be thinking that this was a rich man's school, but you would be wrong. West Patent was nestled in the town of Bedford, with two affluent neighborhoods to the east and two working class neighborhoods to the west. We were the "catch-all" school—different in every way. Our student population comprised kids who lived in shelters, and kids whose families included the Kennedys and the top brass of Fortune 500 companies. We were the land of the Haves and the Have Nots, living each day in a place where it simply did not matter.

We spent our days teaching, but we spent our lives planning. We didn't know it at the time, but we were experiencing the beauty of the Hum—that time when everyone and everything is symbiotic. We spent long hours in and outside of school writing curriculum, searching for materials to bring our teaching to life, experimenting with the latest while preserving what we thought was the greatest. We lived and breathed our work in a nontraditional way. Our families became each other's families and our lessons were always important. It went along that way until . . .

New York State decided that everyone needed to account for one-size-fits-all learning.

The intentions of the long arm of government might have been to improve the education of many, but the ignorance placing the laws blindly (or not so blindly) reduced the experience for others. The short-sightedness of those in charge was infuriating.

It started with the introduction of statewide English Language Arts exams for fifth graders. I clearly remember our principal placing the preview format of the first exam in 1991 on the overhead transparency machine at a faculty meeting. Similar to sticker shock, we were stunned by the price we would have to pay to prepare our students for this first step into the world of state assessments.

None of us disputed the need for, and value of, assessments—they allowed us to gain information about where our students fell on a continuum of standards. Of course, we understood this. We also welcomed accountability. In fact, we had been developing portfolios of our students' learning that charted each year's worth of authentic learning opportunities. Large accordion folders held teacher and student selections of work that provided evidence of learning in all areas of the curriculum. The gems nestled in these portfolios captured both teacher and student reflections of how each piece represented a sample of both best and least-developed pieces of work. No one could say that our students, or we, weren't accountable. We set standards infinitely higher than those the state envisioned for our students—and achieved them.

One might wonder why it mattered to us if our standards were truly higher. Wouldn't it be easy for our students to take these tests and do well if more was required from them in their everyday learning? It sounds logical, my dear readers, but teaching and learning just doesn't work like that. With the new laws, we found ourselves spending more and more hours helping students understand a format of testing that neither tested their knowledge by its content nor its format. Pages of multiple-choice questions based on a common reading passage flew in the face of our philosophy.

We believed, as most true educators do, that we should take students from where they were. We worked to raise their level of learning piece by piece with an emphasis on individual needs and attention. No one was reading the same book at the same time in the same way. Do adults all know the same things at a certain age merely because it is written that they should? Doesn't it matter more that our body of knowledge grows as we do and our job as educators is to monitor that pace and provide opportunities that engage students in their own learning? We looked at progress over time and we valued the time it took for young minds to develop. We stood witness to years and years of students achieving success, all in their own way and their own time.

I remember our outcries to the powers above demanding a visit to our school, to our district. "Come spend a day with us and see how we assess our students. Come see how account-able we are. See our success before you make grandiose decisions that meld those who thrive with those who don't into one unrecognizable group of mediocrity." Surely, one visit would convince them that we could be exemplars of effec-tive learning. Surely, one visit would make them want to pick our brains about how students learn. Surely, they would under-stand that we stood among many who devoted their lives to this work. We were not merely teachers—we were one with what we did!

But no one came.

No one answered our cries.

Instead, one regulation after another was passed, and enforced.

Soon we made the decision not to remain a multi-age institution. We were the same teachers with the same passion, but it became so much harder to plan curriculum according to concepts. We were required to be focused on specific content at specific times, and it was simply too difficult and counterproductive to proceed as we had. For example, teaching how simple machines work dovetailed well with the advent of the Industrial Revolution, but one was part of a fourth-grade curriculum and one was fifth grade. So, instead of students building their own inventions to meet the demands of a changing society at the turn of the century, they now learned these concepts and skills in isolation. Not the end of the world but certainly less meaningful and rich. And why? Because the assessments dictated the content.

The erosion of the Hum continued as a rock sliding down a cliff. There was less time and incentive to plan curriculum as a team and more of a need to plan how we would get to the finish line and prepare students for the format of the assessments. We never paid much attention to the actual taking of the tests, but we couldn't leave our students in a compromised position due to our failure to familiarize them with the format and skills needed to take them. So, teaching became a constant tug-of-war between patiently meeting their needs at their individual levels and pushing those trains to move faster on the track.

The thinking that most infuriated me, though, was the message we received from New York State gurus that the assessments were "meant to help us address student needs and not to be used to rank them." Really? Tell me, then, how is it that the tests were taken in January but results not received until late July? How did this inform our teaching for the school year in which the tests were taken?

Also, why were students scored from 1-4 with a score of 2 requiring proof of remediation? We wasted so much precious time discussing the difference between a "low 2" and a "high 2," and how the students' performance in February was probably not applicable the following September. Hard to find a Hum in that!

The "taking down the Hum" process might not have been the result of a conspiratorial plot or part of some divine plan, but it had the same effect as Newton's theory that what goes up must come down.

It hit home for me when our recent graduates returned to tell us that they would never forget the Hudson River Unit, a six-week multidisciplinary unit designed around a single book, *Owl's Journey*, written by a local author, Maura Shaw. This gold mine of material allowed us to travel the history of Dutchess County in New York State while learning how to dredge a river, recreate the first circus in the country, write music, and calculate mileage from one end of the county to the other. It was our best work—hand-written, lovingly crafted, and a model of learning as fun, experimental, and individualized. So, you can imagine our sadness when we looked at our ex-students and shook our heads. "We aren't able to do that unit anymore."

It hit even harder the day Nolan showed up. A wiry, tall student from years before, Nolan stood proudly in front of me and shared his success with a New York City theater group, where he cut the competition for a coveted spot in their ensemble. Nolan was our living proof of success. One might have thought of him as a Have Not when he was on Team IV. He lived on the grounds of an estate where his father worked. The estate owner's son also attended our school and there were years when they shared the same classroom.

In some ways, Nolan seemed more fortunate than his counter-part, who went home each day to babysitters, dinners without his parents, and summers spent away from family and home. (Fortunate, yes, but not entirely happy.) Nolan went home each day to a home-cooked meal, a mother who grilled him thoroughly about his day and took long walks with him to exercise his limber and athletic body. School was difficult for Nolan. There were rare after-school dates with friends and his academic skills presented a challenge to him each day.

Then the Team IV magic happened. Each year, we hired an artist-in-residence who was an off-Broadway actress and writer. Working under her direction, we had ten days to write, rehearse, and produce a play that reflected the learning of one particular area of the curriculum. One year it was Colonial America, another year it was the Hudson River valley and so on. All 105 students on Team IV participated in the creation of the show. Costumes were merely colored t-shirts with child-made badges on them. We loved Karen, our artist, because she was all about process and less about product. We devoted ten days a year to small-group writing, to dancing and singing homemade songs and dances. She worked with a musician from the theater and he accompanied it all on his trusty old piano. He made tapes of the music so we could practice as we packed up for dismissal or unpacked our bags in the morning. Talk about the dwarfs whistling while they worked! Can you imagine the sound of 105 children singing as they prepared the start and end of their day?

When the show was done on this particular year, Karen told us she wanted to talk about Nolan. She had been watching him. She noticed his athletic build and created a dance for him. His ideas when writing the script were inventive and inspirational. He was not grounded in practicality; he soared with spirit and originality. She saw that little "something" in him and wanted to help him get involved in theater. It was because of Karen and our opportunity to design curriculum that both taught the concepts we needed to teach and also allowed the learning to be expressed in a multidimensional manner that Nolan was standing before me on that day many years later!

Sadly, I shared that "we weren't able to do that anymore." In that moment, I realized that the Hum had gone away.

It made me think about what else had gone away, what else we were no longer able to do. How had it all happened right under our noses? Could we have fought more? The realization and dismay followed me from my life as a teacher through my life as a principal, and it continues today. If we were humming-birds, those making decisions about what sustains us were pages out of a new text entitled *To Kill A Hummingbird*.

So, on this day when I sit in my warm and loving hair salon, one that I frequent twice a week because I have decided that this is the best present I can give to my aging self, I remember the Hum. I remember it because I am an observer in this shop and I can see it today, a day that is quieter than usual and when all the moving parts of what make this salon what it is are highly synchronized. I see it in their camaraderie, their little jokes and passing smiles. It's a compliment to Gabriel, for the Hum does not merely happen. It's built on creating a team of people who believe in their work, believe in the principle that are all "owners" and not "renters." They are all important parts of a whole and with the absence of one, the work might continue but its heart is compromised.

The thing about the Hum is that no one appreciates it until it is gone. We often call these the good old days, but this is not what they are. Not all old days are good and not all good days contain this symbiotic beat. It's subtle, it's quiet, and it's contained within those rare moments in time when the activities of our lives mirror the moving parts of a well-oiled clock. Each movement on the wheel turns to energize the next movement until a chime is produced precisely when it is supposed to and with the clarity for which it was designed.

Team IV had that Hum until the interference of others who did not take the time to listen to our subtle tune made it difficult to sustain. And yes, I do look back with great fondness for those golden days of education. I'm sad when I gather with my teachers for one of our post-retirement get-togethers and hear the flatness in their voices. Voices that once were lilted, as teachers' voices should be, are now "bummed out" because the Hum they experienced is gone.

If our state and federal governments could see that the before-and-after pictures are skewed, they would understand that increased test scores might measure drilled skills, but don't capture learning. They would hold us accountable for the richness of a good learning experience, not for the students' ability to answer multiple choice questions or write a short answer essay to an unrelatable reading passage. Students who are drilled to do well on these tests do well. Teachers drill them to do well because the stakes are high for the students, the teachers, the individual schools, and the school districts. It really isn't the assessments themselves that are so bad, but the status they have in defining what successful students and teachers are. (And don't get me started on the fact that the company that won the bid in New York State to write the assessments is the same company that publishes and markets preparation and remediation materials to the schools. Hmm. Do we have an incentive to succeed here?)

So, the kids who grow up in a school without the Hum may never know what they are missing. It doesn't matter if they are a Have or a Have Not. The ramification of raising children in an environment where the stakes are too high, and the journey of learning is not appreciated, affects them all. I am not talking about performance, as many are performing well. Those who aren't are injected with remedial programs and services until they do. We praise their performance and so sadly lose sight of the "out of the box" talents and abilities they bring to the table.

My thoughts return to Gabriel and the wonderful Hum he has created. He is too busy creating it to notice it, as is often true when the Hum is finely tuned and right. I so desperately want to celebrate this with all of them, but it is not mine to celebrate. As Roseanna towel dries my hair and heats the flat iron, I say a little prayer that my special group of friends experiences many more years of today. It is a gift they have earned, and it will one day be presented to them as they look back on their lives and understand the tune they so magically and excellently played.

CHAPTER TWELVE

Broken Pieces

It started with a flyer that my friend Mona had picked up from a local craft show. "Would you have any interest?" she asked as we talked about ways to make the upcoming fall and winter more interesting.

"Hmmm, not sure," I responded. "Remember how the pottery class went? Not much of an artist. But I do like stuff like that. Okay, let's find out about it."

A few months later, we found ourselves seated in a small art studio, marveling at the work on display. "Oh boy," I said. "I'll never be able to do that!" Mona looked at me and giggled, for we had both been down this road before—the search for artistic expressions that might turn out to be the one we had talent for.

There was the time we had tried our hands at pottery. Does every newly retired person do that? Disaster doesn't even begin to describe it. Somehow I didn't feel "at one with the wheel," and my hand-carved creations, well . . . let's not go there.

From that, we moved on to jewelry making. The beads looked pretty when we strung them onto necklaces and bracelets, but in the light of day, well, let's just say we made them at day camp, you know what I mean?

Then we decided to become a bit more intellectual and try our hand at Bridge. I actually liked it! But eventually the rules and conventions got too complicated for my brain and I didn't like the feeling of stupidity that came along with every tournament.

So, there we were at Wishflower Studio, whimsically named and owned by a very talented lady named Libby. Libby's studio is the kind of place where one feels instantly comfortable. A condensed space next door to the Mamaroneck Chamber of Commerce in a crowded industrial park, one would scarcely notice it. But once you find it, you're lured back to it over and over again, like a puppy returning a ball to his owner, knowing there's more fun on the way.

We signed up for two sessions totaling seven hours of instruction, guidance, and materials, but what we got was so much more.

"Let me show you around," smiled Libby. "This is the studio where we work, but back here is where the goodies are." Stepping into a long, narrow room, Mona and I felt dazzled by the array of colors and textures set before us, much like children in an old-fashioned penny candy store. Flashbacks of a simpler time likened the polished stones and buttons to the strips of candy dots that dominated the walls of Henny's Pennies, the store I frequented as a child with the money I saved from random gifts of coins from my brother or parents. Slabs of stained glass brought me back to the windows of my childhood synagogue, where I watched in wonder how the sun peered in, making congregants' hair turn varying shades of blue and green. There was no end to the shelves piled high with pieces of pottery, broken ceramic dishes, handles from teapots, and assorted large chunks and tiny bits of pottery. I imagined I was inside a kaleidoscope. Everywhere I turned I was met with more colors and shapes.

"What kind of piece do you think you want to make?" asked Libby. "I have picture frames here, as well as mirrors you can decorate. Or if you want, you can make a tray like the ones over here. I would suggest saving the cookie jars for next time, once you get the idea of how to do it, but if you really want to make one I will help you."

Mona and I each picked a tray as our first project—something flat and not too difficult. Libby handed us plastic containers to use for placing materials we wanted to use. It was dizzying to navigate her drawers of beads, chains, and stones, as well as the choices in colored glass and tiles! Little by little, with painstaking thought, I chose a palette of blue for my beach house tray. I selected rocks with sayings on them, tiles and glass stones with varying textures to design what I thought might be a fanciful piece of art.

Container in hand, I approached a stool at the studio table. Two women had already taken their seats there, both with expertly designed pieces in front of them. *Oh boy—I will never be able to do that!*

How often had I said this in my life? I wondered. *I will never be able to do that!* Like the gun that sounds at the start of a race, these were always my fighting words. *I will never be able to pass this test.* But I did. *I will never be able to work and raise a family.* But I did. I will never be able to get a teaching job. But I did. *Become a principal, write a book, marry Mark, survive his death* . . . well, somehow, I did it.

But I still felt, with the utmost certainty, that whenever a new challenge came my way, I would not be able to conquer it. *Maybe it is time to change this mantra,* I thought. *Should I start with mosaics or with losing those five pounds?*

Sensing my hesitation, Libby encouraged me to start placing materials on the tray to form a design. She assured me that the design would come once I began. *Where have I heard that before?* My wonderful editor, Rebecca, told me that many times. "Just write. It will come."

Soon I was marveling at how much fun it was to cut glass the way Libby showed us. Using tools that were unfamiliar and wearing goggles that made me feel like a pro, I felt myself sliding into a comfort zone. My shoulders began to relax as I softly hummed along to the James Taylor music playing in the background. The Zen feeling in the room was palpable.

Libby showed us the glue we needed to use to paste our pieces to our trays. We faced the next challenge of cutting up pieces of glass to fit between the spaces left behind. Five hours had passed, and we had done all we could for that day. Five hours of no phone calls, no email—nothing but music, soft chatter, cutting glass, gluing tiles, and exchanging compliments.

As I waited the two days before our return, I found my thoughts wandering to Libby and Wishflower Studio. Sitting on the New York City subway, grateful to have a seat in the can of sardines that transported me to and from my city haunts, I yearned for the peacefulness of the day I had spent there. *Ugh! Doesn't the guy hanging over me as he holds onto the bar know what deodorant is? What's with that woman singing and bopping at a rapid-fire pace to music no own else hears?*

Funny how it never bothered me before, the beat of New York. Even the raucous sound of my grandchildren at play, something I usually enjoyed, suddenly seemed harsh and invasive. *Do they really have to chase each other all day with high-pitched voices and screams loud enough to stop a train in its tracks?* I just couldn't wait to go back to the new place I had discovered.

I wanted to bathe in the sunlight streaming into the studio, become enveloped in the music and people I found there, and see what my creation would become. On that day I learned how to grout and polish my tray. Libby celebrated by taking pictures, and I returned home with my first masterpiece and what I knew would become a new passion.

My weekly visits to Wishflower have become increasingly important and precious to me. I usually start by staring at the walls of tile and glass, wondering what to create. As I work, I find my mind often drifting to Mark.

I've survived six long years without his physical presence. I have felt very much like the broken pieces of mosaics lying before me. My life has been a piece of my children and grandchildren, a piece of my mother, a piece of friends, and a piece of writing, but I see myself in the center of this universe with arms upstretched to the sky, trying to coax each part down to a canvas in which I can form a cohesive picture. Mark was the grout that tied it all together and without him my life has been floating in space.

Now here I am, having found, ironically, a place in a mosaic studio where the primary goal is to place fragments together to create something new and special. Amid all these pieces in front of me, I realize and finally accept that I am now the glue. I am holding it all together now. I can bring down these floating pieces of my life. I have the power and I have the ability.

I hear the soft background music of James Taylor singing "Fire and Rain." The lyrics leap out as he sings ". . . sweet dreams and flying machines in pieces on the ground." I sigh and turn my thoughts back to my newest creation. Those flying machines aren't going to be rebuilt, but maybe I can make a trivet. I'm something I haven't been in a long time: I'm hopeful.

I've begun to take myself seriously. I no longer say "I'm going to mosaics today." Instead, I say "I'm working at the studio today." My seriousness has nothing to do with a desire to be an artist—it's about making a shift from a "broken to pieces" kind of life to a "broken pieces coming to life" kind of life.

Where did I once read that "there's a crack in everything— that's how the light gets in"? I see myself gluing the fragments of my past and present life into whatever new creation I'm working on in the studio, but also see that there's space for expressing who I am at this moment in time, as well as my dreams for tomorrow. I see it in the bright colors I choose. I see it in my choices of textures and mediums. I'm beginning to understand more about myself from my time at Wishflower than years of therapy could ever do.

I see that I actually enjoy the unevenness of my creations. I don't make symmetrical pieces; I like the imperfections of my work more than I do the rest. I'm comfortable with that, and I realize that this has been the pattern of my life. Never the straight path. Never the easy way. Mostly happy, but the unhappy times were born from extreme situations that most people I know have not experienced.

Mark often old me I was a survivor and I never really liked that distinction. While I always felt that being a survivor wasn't bad, the fact that I've had to be, over and over again, is. But I'm beginning to believe that what I now need in order to survive is me. Me on my own and not propped up by anyone or anything else, no matter how much I love whom or what the prop is. The old tapes in my head challenge me by calling me back to a life I can no longer live. But, increasingly, those tapes are being put on the shelf to be called upon for a memory and not a mandate.

And, yes, time with Libby in Wishflower studio is helping me do that. Just as the time I've spent with Rebecca in chronicling my story has helped me. A double irony! It wasn't happenstance that compelled me to search the Internet that wintry night two years ago looking for a writing coach. I could have picked anyone, but I was supposed to pick Rebecca. And it is

Rebecca who took that lead, who pulled me along with her whispers . . . *Just write and the story will come.*

My despair took the shape of words that she helped me piece together. My writing with Rebecca became the protective cocoon in which I could safely express my thoughts in order to emerge as a stronger and freer self. At the moment I felt that cocoon opening, Libby appeared to meet Rebecca's push, and pulled me into an alternative world of making the broken whole again.

Just write and the story will come.

Just start and the picture will come.

The writing and the search for artistic expression have come from a place deep within my soul. It has been my call to survive, to express my subconscious understanding that I am human, and as a human I need to extract meaning from all that I experience. We know that humans have an innate instinct to survive. But how can we survive if we can't ascribe meaning to the challenges that cross our paths? As this meaning becomes clearer to us, it is also human instinct to express it in a way that communicates to others what these experiences have been. Words, tiles—it's all the same. They're merely my markers along the path, telling me I survived.

That's the thing about being engulfed in grief: All you see is the darkness, all you want is what you can't have, and all you hope for is the past. I needed six years to walk through that tunnel and two years to write my way out of it. I can see color again. I see the possibility of bringing what was mine with me into a new world that has room for more. I needed those Ambien nights, the delusions about people I didn't know, the quest to see Mark in every person who shared his genes or even knew him, the search for signs in ladybugs and butterflies. I needed those mallard ducks to appear in my brook. I even needed the rage I felt toward my mother and the ladies of La Maison. I needed Wyatt, I needed Pete, and I needed Melvyn. I needed those roses in bloom whether or not I noticed them. I even needed that six-ounce can of pineapple juice. I didn't want any of it, but I needed it all.

CHAPTER THIRTEEN

The Jack I Knew

A hush came over the courtroom as the German psychiatrist began to shout in a heavily accented voice. His eyes bulged, and his stance was reminiscent of a cross between Albert Einstein and the Nutty Professor. "The research on Zoloft is now well-documented as to its effects on judgment! Temporary insanity has been seen in more than fifty subjects who have . . . "

Good G-d, I thought, would someone please stop this man?

It was October 1999—two years after Jack's murder. It had taken two long years to bring Dick Schulman to trial. Dick Schulman, the man who killed my brother, Jack, and his business partner, Howard, in cold blood one late afternoon in August 1997.

On the evening of August 5, Tina was away at college, Erika was doing her high school homework, and Mark was still at work. I was forty-five years old. As I prepared to leave for a meeting at our synagogue where I was a board member, the phone rang. I had just grabbed my car keys to leave, so I was tempted to let the answering machine get the call, but I saw that it was from my sister-in-law, and something inside summoned me to answer anyway. Darcy's voice was calm and low. "Robyn, Jack was involved in an altercation at his office this afternoon and he didn't make it."

How does one process this? "What about my parents?" I said, before any pain or feeling set in. "Do they know? Where are they?" I had to call Mark. I really had no idea what I was supposed to do.

It took two long years for us to get to trial—two agonizing years of waiting. But finally, here we were: Mark, my parents, my sister-in-law, and my fifteen-year-old niece. We sat together on the hard bench in that cold courtroom in Boston, Massachusetts, trying to hold ourselves together while my poor niece learned for the first time how unfair and unpredictable life could be. I squeezed Mark's hand with unusual tightness. What a rock he was!

"The evidence Dr. Gershorn has presented on Zoloft is disputable and undocumented," objected Susan, the assistant district attorney. "Motive has already been established by the court. The business was undergoing a reorganization. Mr. Schulman was unhappy. He was worried about not being able to sustain his lifestyle under this reorganization. This is not about temporary insanity. This is about a disgruntled businessman who killed his partners! Zoloft or not, he planned it, orchestrated it, spoke about it with precision and clarity. The trunk of his car held an array of weapons . . . "

As her voice melted into the background, my reverie began. Could this be my Jack that they were referring to? I wasn't privy to his business dealings, but I knew that Jack's entire life had revolved around being everyone's hero. He would have more likely tried to save someone than destroy them. Jack was a giver, not a taker. I smiled as I remembered . . .

The doorbell rang as I arranged my seventh-grade math papers across the small kitchen table of our apartment. My strawberry Pop Tart popped out of the toaster at the same time the doorbell rang. I retrieved the pastry and returned to the table, forgetting about the doorbell. I wasn't that keen on answering doorbells when I was home alone anyway. I was a responsible twelve-year-old and usually obeyed the house rules. "Do not open the door unless you know who it is!" But I was home alone a lot, so that rule got broken once in a while.

BZZZ, BZZZ!

Who is this relentless person? I thought. I wanted to start my homework because I knew it would be hard and take a long time.

Ugh! The hand on the buzzer was unending.

BZZZ, BZZZ, BZZZ . . . *Enough!*

I opened the peephole on the door and saw no one. Yet the buzzer was still beeping. *Maybe it's stuck?* I opened the door to look. The doorbell stopped, but no one was there. *Oh well.* As I started to close the door, I spotted it propped against the doorframe: A big red bow on it, just sitting there looking pretty.

"Oh my G-d!" I said aloud. I looked around but saw no one. I picked up the odd-shaped, oversized package and brought it inside. *Who could have left this here?* I wondered. *Maybe they got the wrong apartment. But look how beautiful it is!*

BZZZ, BZZZ! *Now what?*

I opened the door again to find a second package with a red bow on it—same shape as the first one. *Oh boy, this is getting weird.* I tentatively picked it up and brought it inside.

BZZZ, BZZZ! Again.

I opened the door for the third time to see my seven-teen-year-old brother grinning in the doorway. "Like it?" was all he said.

Confused, I furrowed my brow and looked at him. "What is this for?" I finally asked.

"It's for you. I wanted you to have it."

Tears welled up in my eyes as I stood stunned and overcome with what he had done. My overprotective, argumenta-tive, hulk of a brother had bought me a guitar. For months I had been begging my parents to let me play an instrument. I wanted piano lessons, but we were never going to have a piano. I must have mentioned a guitar. My hero! How many weeks of his clerking at the supermarket did it take for him to do this?

I jerked to attention and looked around the courtroom. *Disgruntled business partner?* The suggestion that the use of Zoloft or dissatisfaction with a business transaction justi-fied murder made my blood boil. How often did Jack have things not turn out for him as planned? He never killed anyone because of it.

The trial for Jack's murder was in its third week, and I vacil-lated from intense focus to dazed and daydreaming. Mark grabbed my hand and gave it a reassuring squeeze. I squeezed his hand back and turned my gaze to the newest witness on the stand, Dick Schulman's mother.

"Richard wasn't this person! Only something terrible would drive him to commit such an act. Even as a young child, Dick was the most compassionate child. He was a good boy!"

Good boy, bad boy. *How ironic,* I thought. The "good boy" committed murder. The "bad boy" that Jack was *told* he was, didn't. Jack was scolded incessantly for not getting straight As and not keeping his closet neat. Dick's mother apparently felt he had a need to carry guns around and use them. Who is to say who is good or bad?

Yet, even as I breathed anger and contempt, I felt a gush of compassion for this woman whose son had committed such a hideous crime. How could I blame her for remembering her son in a way she needed to in order to survive what he had done? After all, we're not born bad, are we?

Jack and I were inseparable throughout my childhood. Sharing a bedroom with a brother who was five years older had its advantages. He was good at having fun and I was good at following him. Sometimes he hid Pepsi and cookies behind the dressers in our room. When our lights were off for the night, he retrieved the Pepsi and tuned in to the Dinah Shore show on the television console that separated our beds. No sound needed because we could hear it from the TV in our parents' room. We had a good party on more nights than one, taking swigs of Pepsi and watching the top talents of the time.

We were a perfect pair. I was the good girl who worked hard in school and kept my mouth shut. He was the "bad boy" who thought school was a place to shine, not as an academic, but as a clown and social king. He had a gaggle of friends, while I had few. Jack voiced his anger at all the unfair elements of childhood, while I remained quiet until much later in life. I did his vocabulary work, and he bought me guitars. I babysat to earn money and he confiscated a portion of it for our play fund. Where else were the bottles of Pepsi and cookies going to come from?

Oh, we had our fights! Mostly they took the form of a game. The best one was when we lined up chess pieces on opposite sides of the living room floor. Beside each of us, on opposing teams, stood a bag of rubber bands. At the count of three, the goal was to knock down as many of the opponent's chess pieces as possible until no rubber bands remained. He was a killer at this game and fortunately no eyes were poked out in the process. I still can't decide if it was more fun to play the game or to listen to my mother rant about finding rubber bands behind the living room drapes. Our clean-up was not always perfect, but we weren't exactly lying when we said we played chess after school. As I said, we were alone a lot!

And then there were our special jam sessions. We had a metal trash can in our bedroom that was perfect for amplifying voices. Yes, we had to sing into the garbage can for it to work, but it was a small price to pay for the concerts we gave to each other. His favorite was "The Lion Sleeps Tonight". I was always excited to sing the "wingawetta, wingawetta" refrain while he belted out the verse. He then moved on to "Don Quixote" from *The Man of La Mancha* while I focused on memorizing the soliloquy from *Carousel*. Not sure what the neighbors thought, but no one snitched, so it couldn't have been that bad. As you know, we were alone a lot.

Things did get dicey once when Jack had the brilliant idea of throwing orange peels out the window with a paper clip pierced through the thick skin. Looking back on that one, we could have killed someone, but youth is blind. The sign posted in the elevator about the orange peel incident in the building put us on alert, and we privately laughed when our parents expressed their horror of anyone doing such a thing. It didn't stop us, though. Oranges were cheap back then and we had money in our play fund. Eventually, we heard about the danger this game presented to others and we stopped. No one was the wiser and this is the first time I have admitted to this act of crime.

Jack had wheels and that meant freedom. Not a car, but a maroon red Schwinn with great handlebars or, as I thought of them, my seat. We flew down the streets. No helmets back then, no fears, and no one to stop us. (Did I mention we were alone a lot?) One time, Jack put on the brake a bit too hard and I was dropped from my elevated position on the handlebars to the metal cover of the front tire. It took about a week for my private parts to heal, but I never told. That would have dampened our freedom a great deal. I was mad at Jack for that week—less because of the accident and more because of his evil laugh every day when he saw me limping.

"Robyn, I think you should step out for this part."

Huh?

"Let's go. It isn't necessary for you to see this," said Mark. *What did I miss?* My parents, sister-in-law, and niece were leaving the courtroom.

Susan was about to submit evidence of that gory day. No—I wanted to stay. How could I leave just because it was difficult? Jack's leaving me did not mean I had to leave him. It was too late, anyway. I had already seen the shirt—the blood-soaked white shirt where his heart exploded.

"Robyn, we're going." Mark took my arm and ushered me into the hallway. He was my protector, of course, and I understood, but it made me so sad that someone always had to leave.

Broken hearts, oh yes. I remember the first time I felt my heart explode with sadness. Jack and I were five years apart. The day eventually came when my playmate of a brother packed up to go to college . . . in Oklahoma! Yes, I think that was the first time my heart broke. I cried the whole drive taking him there and the whole way back.

Life was changing for him, and it was surely going to change for me. He took me out for bowling and dinner the night before he left. "Don't worry, squirt. I'll be home a lot and you can always call me. I'll always be the big bad brother looking out for you."

Bad brother? Not to me. If I knew then what I do now, I would have understood this as a marker in how he viewed himself. After all, he had been hearing it for many years.

A poke on the arm, the packing of suitcases, and that was it. I remained a kid, and he went off to become something more than that. I thought I might actually like being on my own for a while. No more big protective brother storming into Baskin-Robbins at 3 p.m. to check what group I was hanging out with or what boy I had my latest crush on. No one picking up the phone extension to tell me I really needed to get back to my homework and stop babbling to my best friend, Margot. But I didn't like this feeling at all. It felt like a band-aid had been ripped off my skin and now I had open wounds with no protection. Protection from what exactly? From being home alone. He was a friend, a comrade, and on the front line to fend off the craziness and unhappiness that was found there. Like the time . . .

"Mom's at it again. It's Sunday, so what do you expect?"

"What?" I groggily asked as I woke up a bit late on one of those infamous days.

"Can't believe you slept through the screaming. She's locked herself in the bathroom again. He's gone downstairs for a walk."

"Mom, I have to pee," I said as I knocked gently. "Can I come in?"

"Where's your father?"

"He went downstairs for a walk."

I heard the click of a lock and before me stood my mother. She stepped aside and I quickly went in and locked the door behind me.

"Tell him I am going out. I'm leaving," she said coldly.

I felt no need to answer. Jack mumbled, "Uh huh" as she grabbed her purse and slammed the door behind her.

Okay, so it was going to be another one of those Sundays. Only G-d knew what the fight was about this time. Jack and I would just have to wait it out before the usual phone call came around 4 p.m. I had homework to do, and we could always play Scrabble. We'd think of something.

My father sat in the club chair in his bedroom watching the football game, where he had been all day, when the call came in. She was at a phone booth in Manhattan, where she had taken the train earlier that day.

"Come home, Barbara. Enough already. I'm sorry. The kids are waiting here." He stubbed out his cigarette. "What time does the train get in? We'll pick you up."

Some muffled talking on the other end before Jack and I were summoned to get on the phone and promise to never do whatever it was we didn't remember doing in the first place. Jack did the talking. I was too young to know what to say.

"I'm sorry. I promise. I won't be bad again," he said sincerely. Off we would go to the train station, then to the Chinese restaurant where we looked like the typical happy suburban family that we weren't. It was as if air had been released from a valve. My parents tried to speak lightly and happily, while no one let on about another long, miserable day home just waiting for the anger to end.

Just another Sunday.

I found myself staring at the man who killed my brother. Everything about him revolted me. He looked unlikeable even if he hadn't committed a crime, with his dark beady eyes, his arrogant expression, and ever-present smirk. He was such a weasel, the way he slinked across the courtroom. A true coward, he didn't find strength in words—only in weapons.

"We will take a fifteen-minute recess and reconvene to question one of the witnesses," said the judge.

Oh, yes, Jack's secretary, Sharon. She testified earlier that day that Jack knew something was wrong as soon as Dick came into the office. As Dick sat across from him with the pistol on his lap, Jack told Sharon, "If Dick isn't gone in thirty seconds, call 911. And I think you should leave the office now." I am sure one of his last thoughts was of protecting her.

Feeling lonely once Jack left for Oklahoma, I dug into my schoolwork to escape my parents' constant screaming and fighting. It all seemed louder now, so I closed what was now my bedroom door and dove into my music, my writing, and a bit of collaging. However, all the distractions in the world couldn't hide the fact that the time and distance between me and one of my very first protectors was growing by the day.

Evidence of this filtered into my life little by little, year by year. Jack did come back, all right, but not necessarily to me. Oklahoma did not turn out to be "OK" and Jack was not equipped to handle his newly gained independence. His first year ended as quickly as it began. He took a job and a small apartment while attending school at night at a college close to home.

Little by little he figured out how to survive, and his focus was less on his little sister and more on negotiating a relationship with our parents as he tried to become his own person. I began to climb the growing-up pole too at this point, and actually got myself ready to start college a year early. I wanted to be the one to leave this time, especially after the past year of Sundays. Or that week when . . .

The argument was big this time. My father had to attend a trade convention in Avalon-by-the-Sea in New Jersey. It was an overnight trip and my mother did not want him to go. He returned to a locked door—chained and impossible to open. He slept in his car in the garage below our apartment building that whole weekend, while I snuck food to him each time I brought laundry to the laundry room in the building's base-ment. It was Mom and me . . . and Dad in the basement. I begged her to let him in when I heard his key at the door. I called Jack to come help.

He wasn't there when my mother opened the door and had me stand between her and my dad. It was then that she made him swear on my life that he would not do whatever it was that he did ever again. We probably had Chinese food that night.

A few months later, just before I started college, Jack announced he was getting engaged.

Not so fast! Wanda was not Jewish, and my mother was unmovable. He became estranged from my parents, particularly my mother, in the months preceding his wedding, and I was forbidden to see him. But, my dear readers, you should know me by now. My father covered for me as I snuck around to see him and to show him and Wanda my support.

The marriage didn't last, but how could it? They never stood a chance. The not-so-invisible umbilical cord was strong— Wanda's religion had nothing to do with their demise. Taffy can only be stretched so far before it finally breaks.

I shrugged this memory off as we began a new day in the courtroom. We began to bring cushions for the hard benches we were seated on for six hours a day. Mark noticed that whenever Schulman was escorted into the courtroom, his hands were cuffed, but he always had a big chair and comfy pillow waiting for him. On this day, however, there was no pillow. Dick looked around for it but eventually parked his bottom on a hard chair. Mark nudged me and pointed to the chair, a sly smile coming over his face.

It didn't sink in at first, but when I turned to him again, I saw the glint in his eye. "What do you know about that pillow?" I asked.

"Not much, except it pays to be here early," he murmured. "They will never find that pillow again, I assure you."

I giggled, which caught my parents' attention. I played the game of telephone and passed the information down the line, and a smile peeked out from the corners of all of our faces. Just this small moment—this small gesture—brought a brief distraction to the nightmare we were living. Mark was the only man I knew who would have noticed the unfairness of Schulman having a pillow while we sat on hard wooden benches. He was also the only man I knew who would have actually done something about it.

It was 1973 and in my family, history was repeating itself. I became engaged to Mark and was instantly denied any joy from my engagement by my unrelenting parents. It wasn't because of religion this time, though. It might have been due to my young age, but the true underlying cause was my mother's inability to relinquish control. Do you remember, "Honey, you can be whatever you want—except Mark's wife"? When my father said that to me, I realized that he didn't really get it after all. I also realized that Jack wasn't going to be able to protect me anymore—he barely had enough energy to protect himself. He didn't call me to provide the same support and reassurance that I provided him just a few years before, listening with full understanding and sympathy as he railed against our parents and the unfairness of it all.

Something had changed in him, and I was hurt. He told me he liked Mark, and he told me I should do what would make me happy, but his actions did not support that. Little by little he began to disappear from my life. I didn't understand his discomfort around Mark. Mark could have been, and would have been, Jack's greatest ally. But Mark's trajectory for success and happiness was simply too much for Jack to take. The more our life together blossomed, the more Jack retreated. Mark started Columbia's School of Business and Public Health, and our marriage did not fail—in fact, our devotion to each other became more intense than ever. This was all too difficult for Jack to accept. He wasn't against us; he simply couldn't stand to be around us.

I noticed and became upset. Why did I not only have to choose between my parents and Mark but now also between my brother and Mark? I knew he was unraveling. He was difficult to be around; he was constantly searching for something. One day he was a police officer, another day he was a school bus driver, one day he was in school, and on another he was starting a business. He became unrecognizable to me, and then he was simply gone.

A part of me understood that he was a man caught in a web between seeking approval from his parents and breaking the cocoon that stunted his growth. He was spinning through space with no safe place to land. The result was his simply choosing to leave.

We made some attempts through the years that followed. We met for lunch, we made promises. We tried to reconnect. His solution was to buy expensive gifts, but all I wanted was time. Little by little, the bond that had tied us together for so many years frayed and then severed. I never believed the love was lost, just the relationship.

Eventually Jack remarried and moved to Massachusetts. He was successful there—a man who dusted himself off over and over until he reached his goal. He had his own business, a happy marriage, and a daughter. He built his white picket fence around a beautiful home, but he never lost that driving need to see the look of approval on our father's face. Nor did he lose the old tapes in his head that told him he wasn't good enough.

He told his wife and daughter that he had played on the football team for Oklahoma University, stopping only when he suffered a knee injury. They believed he graduated from Oklahoma, and that he was originally in the pre-med program. He wasn't. He failed out the first year. But the tragedy to me was that he must have believed they wouldn't have loved him unless these things about him were true. I know they would have. I know they would have loved him without the revised story of his life. They would have loved him without the expensive gifts and lavish parties he liked to host. They appreciated his constant generosity, but they wouldn't have loved him less without it.

He didn't know when he died that just being himself was enough for all of us—even my parents, who made it tough but did love him. He was still rattled by my life, even as it was more modest than his. It didn't help that my parents became my biggest fans and never failed to tell Jack how wonderful we all were. He rarely returned to New York and our kids never became close. There were times when we thought things would change, but they never did.

The injustice of it all was that Jack never had a chance to end his story. He was only forty-eight years old.

If we had more time, he might have mellowed out with age.

If we had more time, he might have stopped bringing home Hondas with red ribbons on them to catch my father's approval.

If we had more time, he might have gained the perspective to see Mark as a friend.

If we had more time, he might have been content.

If we had more time, he might have known he was loved.

I have read and reread the newspaper clippings, seeking answers as to why Dick Schulman took a gun to my brother's head that day. The answer is not in the large type or in the fine print. Just as the answers to my quest to understand why Mark was taken from me too soon were not in the medical reports or books.

Nor have I found an answer to how two parents can love a child so much but still reject the very essence of who he is. Through it all, the unrealistic expectations they had for him, the hopes and dreams they transferred to him, the disappointments they felt, and the blind eye they had for all he was—through all that they loved him, simply because he was theirs. That is the way it is with parents who suffer from narcissistic personality disorder: they love you and reject who you are in the hope of your becoming who they want you to be. At my time in life, as hard as it all was, I came out on the side of two people who did the best they could with what they had at the time. Unfortunately, Jack didn't live long enough to make peace with that.

My quests have eventually brought me to the realization that not all answers are ours to have. Jack's quest in life ended tragically. He never gained any sort of wisdom about the answers he sought. He died without the peace of knowing a life well-lived was the one he had already built. He didn't have the time to clear his head of those voices that told him he wasn't good enough, successful enough, or just enough. He couldn't look out on the landscape of his life to see it through his own eyes and not the eyes of the people who raised him. He never came out of that cocoon.

"All rise. We find the defendant guilty on two counts of murder. Concurrent life sentences with no parole."

October 1999. The verdict came down on an exceptionally clear and cold day. I clutched the pile of rubber bands in my hand and kneeled at exactly the right distance from Jack's headstone. My fingers found their familiar position, I drew back my thumb, and released. The rubber band hit the target straight on.

"We got him, Jack," I said. "He'll never see the light of day again. Schulman is gone. Let it all go, my big brother. Be at peace at last." It only took another moment to lay the pile of unused rubber bands on the smooth, natural stone.

CHAPTER FOURTEEN

The Ladies of La Maison

O*utside door opens. Camera tracks ROBYN's Tieks black flats. She enters a building and stops at the front desk. Conversation can be heard as the camera slowly tracks up from the back of shoes to back of Robyn's head. She is wearing a lightweight navy cotton cardigan over black leggings. Her medium brown hair falls straight upon her shoulders. Over one shoulder Robyn carries a large black Tory Burch tote, papers peeking over the top. Her voice is soft, but one who knows her would detect a slight hint of annoyance.*

ROBYN

    Hi, Carla. How are you doing? Have you seen her today?

Robyn signs her name in book before looking up. Camera reveals Robyn as a sixty-something woman with somewhat soft but tense features.

CARLA

Oh, Robyn. Hi! Good to see you. She looks great! Not a hair out of place, playing her mahjong games. Seems happy to me.

ROBYN

From your lips to G-d's ears, Carla. Thanks. See you later.

The sound of violins playing in the distance. Robyn quickly glances at the daily activity sheet posted in the lobby.

BACK BY POPULAR DEMAND!
WESTCHESTER PHILHARMONIC
1:30 PM | 2ND FLOOR ATRIUM
LIGHT REFRESHMENTS

Robyn walks toward the dining room. Camera follows her down the hall, taking in the nicely furnished corridor strewn with older people chatting, some with walkers, others huddled as back in the olden days when entertainment meant gathering around a desktop radio to hear if Babe Ruth had made that final home run. All smile and greet her as she passes. Robyn scans the menu nicely displayed on a music stand in front of the restaurant.

SOUP OF THE DAY: MUSHROOM BARLEY
CHOICE OF: LAMB CHOPS WITH MINT JELLY,
SWEET PETITE PEAS, MASHED POTATOES
OR
BUTTERFLIED SHRIMP WITH HARICOTS
VERTS, WILD RICE WITH MUSHROOMS

Robyn turns away from the restaurant and approaches the hall leading to her mother's apartment. She smiles at the residents as she passes them and notes their tight-lipped smiles in return. Eyes ahead and fixed on the hallway in front of her, she overhears the whispering comments, "Barbara's daughter." Residents smile and nod their heads in approval as she passes.

GLORY

Oh, hi, Miss Robyn! Your mother will be so happy to see you. I was just in her apartment. Always worried about those plants, you know, but they look great.

ROBYN

Thanks, Glory. She loves you, you know. Have a good day!

Robyn smiles to herself and proceeds. A 4' 11" woman, eighty-four pounds soaking wet, walks up the corridor and faces her. She is easily recognizable by the larger-than-her-head Ann Landers hairdo, and the impeccable outfit of black slacks, blue turtleneck (allowed only because it has a nine-inch zipper sewn into the back of it to allow the hair not to get mussed), and black hip-length duster. Her face breaks out into a huge smile as she sees Robyn approach and her hands fly up.

BARBARA

Robyn! Oh my G-d. I am so happy to see you! Come here. We'll go back to the apartment. Did you have lunch? I didn't know you were coming.

Robyn kisses mother on the cheek.

ROBYN

No, Mom. I just needed you to sign these papers for your new bank account. You have mahjong today and I can't stay that long. I see they're having a concert, too. Is that after mahjong?

BARBARA

Those squeaky instruments? No, thanks. I can skip mahjong. I'd rather be with you.

ROBYN

No, no. I'll walk you and you can sign these then.

Cut to game room where groups of seniors are seated at game tables either dealing cards or setting up for mahjong. Robyn and Barbara approach the table where a TALL, SLENDER WOMAN motions to them.

WOMAN

Aren't ya playing, Barbara? We're waiting for you to be the fourth.

Barbara hesitates.

ROBYN
(shouts)
Yes, yes, she is going to play!

(whispers to her mother)
I will stay and watch a little. I need to learn how to play.

BARBARA

You will? Ok. Everyone, you remember my daughter, Robyn? She wants to learn how to play. Let's go.

As Barbara takes her place, Robyn pulls up a chair and smiles at the group as they mix tiles in the center of the table and start to build their walls.

BARBARA

Come closer, Robyn, so you can see my hand.

(whispers in Robyn's ear)

This is called a wall. We each take two tiles at a time and form two rows of 18 tiles in front of our holders, like this.

LYDIA

I am East today.

Lydia, leader of the giraffe group at La Maison. Cloaked in cashmere and pearls, tall and slender, she is loved and feared.

BARBARA

So, East is one of the directions in the game. Whoever is East gets to start the game.

(then whispering)

I don't know how she got to decide that she is East today!

Lydia throws the dice, which lands on four. She takes four tiles and places them in front of her wall.

BARBARA

That's called a hot wall. I'll explain that later. Watch.

Lydia distributes four tiles at a time to each player until each have thirteen tiles on their racks. Robyn observes the women's faces as they contort their mouths to show approval or disdain at the tiles they get. She watches her mother arrange her tiles into clusters of matching pictures while glancing at the mahjong card beside her. All that is heard is the click, click of tiles being moved around the racks. Robyn yawns. Barbara motions to the woman sitting to the right of her.

BARBARA
(whispers)
You remember Beatrice, she likes to be called Bertie?

ROBYN
Yep. Good to see you Bertie.

BERTIE
Hello. Do you remember me? I was a social worker. You worked in Scarsdale. I lived on Herringbone Lane in that house with the big porch. We had five bedrooms, but who needed that when Arthur died!

Bertie is a transplanted city mouse. She wears shades of brown, has cloudy, small brown eyes, and moves in scurrying, staccato rhythms.

BARBARA
(whispers)
If I hear about that big house one more time!

RHODA
Shhh! We aren't going to be able to play if you are going to talk, girls!

Rhoda the rower—one of the beavers. Ninety-two years old, former captain of her alma mama's rowing team and still rows each week at the local gym.

BARBARA
(whispers)
Bertie's just jealous that she doesn't have a
daughter like you. So she had a big house. Big
deal! You know how I didn't want to go into the
hospital the day you were born. I don't know what
I would have done if you weren't a girl.

ROBYN
(stands abruptly and grabs her bag)
Mom, I'll be right back. Need to use the bathroom.

*Robyn walks down the hall and glances at her watch. Robyn
walks into the mailroom and glances at the sign-up sheets
and activity schedule.*

HELLO DOLLY
WEDNESDAY, MARCH 23

*She scans the names on the sign-up. Robyn wanders into the
library. She glances at the bird cage at the entrance.*

ROBYN
Little birds, are YOU happy here?

*Scene shifts to game room as Robyn enters and approaches
the game table. Loud voices are heard as she sees her mother
gathering her things and standing up.*

BARBARA
I told you last week that if you are going to interrupt
our game every week to join the bingoheads then I
am NOT going to play!

RHODA

Barbara, we have substitutes who can fill in. I want to play both games and I have had enough mahjong.

BERTIE

Why do we have to go through this every week? Can't they change the time for bingo so we can finish the game? I don't understand . . .

RHODA

Then why don't YOU go and ask? Why do I have to be responsible for it all the time? I am going to bingo. See you later girls.

Rhoda shakes her head of gray curls, still wet from her earlier rowing sessions, as she heads toward the adjoining game room.

BARBARA
(to Robyn)

Come to the apartment. I don't want to be here right now. Good-bye everyone.

As Barbara grabs her handbag, Lydia looks her up and down.

LYDIA

See you at dinner, Barbara. By the way, lovely necklace!

Robyn and Barbara enter apartment.

BARBARA

I am not playing on Wednesdays anymore! You saw what happened. Every week. This doesn't happen with my Monday game. Bingo! That's all they want to do.

ROBYN

Has anyone spoken to Stephanie? She can schedule it differently, maybe.

BARBARA

We spoke to her and she said too many people want to play bingo so they now have it four times a week. If they start later, it interferes with the early dinner seating. It's fine. I'd rather not go anyway.

ROBYN

Hmm. Ok. Well, Anyway, I have those papers for you to sign before I go.

BARBARA

I'm making tea. Do you want tea? Sit down. Come in here and sit down. I need you to fix my iPad again. I have this mail to show you. Sit down. What do you want with the tea?

ROBYN

No, Mom. No tea. Thanks.

BARBARA

Of course you're having tea. Do you want coffee? Sit down. I'm making bagels.

ROBYN

No bagels for me. It's 3:00.

BARBARA

Let me go to the bathroom. I'll be right back.

Robyn wanders from room to room of the bright two-bedroom apartment. Everything in its perfect place. Her father's and brother's pictures grin at her from their place on the table.

ROBYN
(aloud to the pictures)
What are you looking at? I'm the last man standing, so I get to do it my way. I'm doing my best, you know. What are you smiling at, Dad? I know, I know, I hear you. "This too shall pass." That's not the answer.

BARBARA
(calls from the kitchen)
Where did you go? Come get your tea. Sit down.

As the two sit at the round table covered by the fitted plastic tablecloth, Robyn places a pen and two papers in front of her mother to sign.

ROBYN
So, Mom, this paper gives me permission to access your account online or on the phone if we ever need to. This other paper officially closes the savings account and transfers the money to checking. Is this all okay?

BARBARA
You know I will do whatever you tell me. I wouldn't be ALIVE if you weren't here.
(crying begins)
Do you know how it feels to sit here and look at that chair? Your father's chair?

ROBYN

Yes, I do, actually.

BARBARA

(getting up to get a tissue)

Every time I look at those great grandchildren, I think about what he missed.

ROBYN

I know. But at least he got to know them all. I wish . . .

BARBARA

I KNOW! Don't you think I know?

ROBYN

Know what, Mom?

BARBARA

(sobbing)

Know how much he would have loved Erika's new house? How he would have loved watching those children at the beach? Don't you think I know? IT IS AN ARROW IN MY HEART!

ROBYN

Yes, I think you know. I also think we were lucky that Dad lived to ninety-one and was healthy until the end. It hits hard when you say these because I only wish . . .

BARBARA

I KNOW! Don't you think I miss Mark every day? The fact that he isn't here to enjoy it? I KNOW!!! I am your MOTHER. I KNOW!

ROBYN

Yep, well what can I say?

Silence. Robyn jolts to attention. She notices her leg shaking back and forth—a telltale sign that she should get going. Mark's voice echoes in her ear. "Stop shaking. Why are you shaking?"

BARBARA

Can you fix the stuff on my iPad?

Robyn picks up her mom's iPad and turns it on. The phone rings. Barbara answers.

BARBARA

Hello. Oh, hello Shirley. Robyn is here. How did you make out at the doctor?

Barbara's voice trails off as Robyn opens the iPad to scan the emails and messages sitting there. She pauses at the pictures taken in Florida of Barbara's three sisters sitting outside the Kravis Center for Performing Arts in West Palm Beach. Barbara is deep in conversation on the phone, so Robyn takes a moment to study the pictures.

ROBYN

Look at all of you: ninety-four, ninety-two, and eighty-one. How is it that the three of you survived your husbands and manage to live your own lives? Look at you—ninety-four with a boyfriend! Traveling, cooking, LIVING! What happened to her. Why not her?

BARBARA

Okay, Shirley, I'll call you tonight. Tell my sisters good-bye for me.

ROBYN

Okay, I downloaded all the pictures from Florida and Ohio and deleted the junk mail. I'm going to get going now. Besides, you have to get ready for dinner.

BARBARA

Ugh—another meal in that dining room! It's a disaster in there and I'm sick of the food. I don't think I want to go down tonight. After all that nonsense with bingo, who needs to see anyone?

ROBYN

Come on, walk me to the lobby. I think the menu had shrimp tonight—a nice change, sounds good.

BARBARA

Not the way they make it. Forget it. I'll walk you. One night we'll go for Chinese.

ROBYN

Yes, we will.

As Robyn and Mom approach the lobby, a group of women are huddled in the hall. They include Lydia, Bertie, and Rhoda. They look up as Robyn and her mother approach and wave them over. Lydia steps forward, glances sideways at the woman closest to her as she rolls her eyes upward.

BARBARA

(whispers as Lydia approaches)

Oh—there's Ellen. Lydia has no more patience for her since she started to forget whatever you tell her. It's very hard. For everyone!

LYDIA

Oh, hi there. Barbara, are you coming to hear the speaker upstairs? He wrote some sort of book about the history of pop music in America.

BARBARA

(with a half laugh)

Think I'll skip it. You can fill me in.

(Lydia turns to Robyn and pulls her aside)

LYDIA

She never comes, but it's wonderful she has you. It has been so hard for her. This place, you know, well—what's the use of complaining? Your father was such a good man. She told me of all the wonderful things they did together.

ROBYN

Oh really? Well. That's interesting.

LYDIA

So whaddya gonna do, right? Here we are in this place.

ROBYN

Tell me, Lydia, what exactly is it about this place? Maybe a change can be made if all of you were more specific about what you don't like.

LYDIA

No, no, dear. It isn't that. What choice do we have? It's hard for you to know. Living without our husbands—well, we just have to make do. I hope it is better for you when you are older, dear. We have to create a whole new life for ourselves. What does your husband do?

ROBYN

My husband passed away a few years ago.

LYDIA

Yes! Your mother did tell us that. What a shame. Then you know how it goes but at least you are young and . . .

Robyn takes a step back and looks toward her mother, who is talking with Ellen.

ROBYN

Yes, well, Lydia I hope you enjoy the lecture. I need to get going.

LYDIA

(takes a step closer to Robyn and whispers)
You spend fifty years with someone and in a minute it's over. You find yourself here . . .

Robyn looks down as she interrupts Lydia mid-sentence.

ROBYN

I know. I'm sorry, Lydia, I gotta run.

Robyn walks toward the front desk in the lobby to sign out.

ROBYN
(calls over to her mother)
I'll speak to you tomorrow, Mom.

BARBARA
Call me later!

Robyn walks out of the building and down the steps leading to the parking lot. Once in her car, she rips off her cardigan and leans back in the driver's seat, letting out a big sigh. She sits for a moment before turning on the ignition. Robyn's hand adjusts the mirrors and rolls down the window.

ROBYN
I can't breathe.

After a moment, she drives down the winding driveway, away from La Maison. The familiar feeling of shaking off a second skin comes over her and she finds herself pulling over to the shoulder of the exit road. She pounds on the steering wheel and starts to weep. Long, hard weeping before she looks up to speak aloud.

ROBYN
I hate this! I hate it all! I hate feeling cold and mean. I hate being here. I hate the lies, the deception of who we are. What do you want now? What do you want from me? Leave me alone! Leave me alone! I am doing the best I can. I'm sorry that it is this way. I'm sorry Dad died. I'm sorry you are living alone in a bird cage. I'm sorry I don't have the key to unlock it. I'm sorry for everything I think and say. But I can't help you today. I'm not even sure I love you today.

Robyn starts to gag. Continues.

ROBYN

Stop telling me that I am everything to you! I shouldn't be. I don't want to be. You want me in that birdcage with you, but I will never go there. I AM SORRY, BUT I WILL MAKE SURE I HAVE A CHOICE! I will NOT be that person to my kids. I just can't, I just can't . . . please G-d, I just can't.

CHAPTER FIFTEEN

Dear Mark

The warmth of the mid-May sun soothed my chilled body as Cyndi pulled away from my driveway with a smile and a wave of her hand. She opened her window and offered a reassuring cheer. "This will be great!"

I watched her car disappear and mumbled, "Yeah, great." Turning to go back inside the house, I paused to gaze at the blossoming Japanese specimen cherry trees, the newly planted gardenias, and the manicured lawn and walkway Mark and I worked so hard to grow. It certainly is beautiful, I thought. Shivering despite the heat of the day, I entered the house and leaned on the closed door behind me.

Now what?

Instinctively I walked upstairs to the office above the garage. This was what a builder would call a bonus room, but it was a very central part of our life here. My workstation was situated on one side and Mark's was on the other. I would sit on my side writing lesson plans and teacher evaluations while Mark labored over financial investments, bills, and sundry household matters.

What a great office, I thought upon entering the room. I looked down at the newly signed contract in my hand. On the top line was written, "Robyn S. Lane, Seller; Cyndi Griffin, Realtor." I sat at Mark's desk.

Where was Mark's signature, his stamp of approval and agreement to sell? One more reminder that I was alone on this journey. Not at all like our other moves where we signed, looked at each other, and felt a spark of excitement at a mutual decision to do something new. Flying solo was much scarier. Remember James Taylor and the mosaic class? "Sweet dreams and flying machines in pieces on the ground."

Well, if I could pull it together then, I can do it again now.

Jerking to attention, I pulled out a legal-sized yellow pad from the top drawer of Mark's desk. *Need to start a list, need to start a list.* Organize the move. Compartmentalize it in a tidy box and deal with it.

I heard a small gasp escape my mouth as I looked at the writing on the pad. Instead of a blank yellow page, I found the last of Mark's scribblings. His funny handwriting greeted me with crooked numbers and almost illegible notes about bills, reminders, and whatnot. Almost seven years later and I still could not discard evidence of his being. Not his handwriting, not his clothes, not the contents of his night table.

I stood and walked over to the large walk-in closet we built for additional office storage. Lined across the walls and shelves remained Mark's suits, shoes, scarves, ties, and coats. The three large red trunks I created were neatly lined up, waiting to be discovered. These were the Treasure Trunks—each one piled with remnants of items that represented Mark in every part of his life. I had attached letters to my grandchildren on each pile with the hope they would one day be interested in discovering the kind of man Papa was.

"Papa liked to carry little items in his jean pockets. This was a rubber part to some tool he picked up somewhere. He would fiddle with it when he was bored or deep in thought. Wasn't he silly?"

"Papa created an amazing health insurance company for people who didn't have money to buy health insurance. It was called Fidelis Care and he helped many, many people in the state of New York. Papa was a smart and kind man."

That would have to be enough. It was time. I was doing the right thing and it was time. Right?

Returning to the desk, I turned to a blank page. It was time to list what items I was going to sell. What should go, what should stay. Who shall live, who shall die? It shall be written. The somber Yom Kippur chant reverberating in my head. *"Who shall live, what should stay? Who shall die, what should go?"* For G-d's sake, this *isn't* life or death; what is wrong with me? Stop it!!

But this pad! Turning once again to the front page I remembered . . .

"Robyn, you need to learn about the finances. What if something happens to me?"

"You promised me nothing was going to happen to you, remember?" I joked.

"I'm serious. You don't know any of this!"

"Because you have this mysterious system that no one can understand. My mind just doesn't work this way."

"I'll explain it. The columns on the pad all have a purpose. I write down all the expenses for the month in this column. I write when each of us get our paychecks for the month here and . . . you're not listening!"

"No, no, I am."

"Forget it. This is absolutely hopeless."

"That's why you do what you do, and I do what I do," I remember stating as I kissed him on the neck and ran off to do something else.

How ironic! Here I sit with the same yellow pad. How can I possibly make a list of what to dispose of on the very same pages Mark used to help us buy these very same things? What would he say?

I felt a panic creep over my body. *Oh my G-d! What have I done? I have to call Cyndi and cancel this. I can't do this! It would be a total betrayal. It is just too hard!*

Running down the stairs to find Cyndi's number, I felt blinded by the sight of our home. A home created for two. The piano where duets were played. Pictures of two in frames. Two desks, a bed where two slept. Seven years of only one in the bed has left one side of the bed higher than the other—startling evidence of a missing partner. An oversized two car garage, his-and-her mugs. Everywhere I looked was a home for two.

Tears and sobs overtook me. There was no self-control, no reasoning with myself. Just long, sorrowful wails escaped my lips as I shrunk to the kitchen floor.

"Please, Mark. I am sorry. I am so, so sorry. I can't do this anymore. Please understand.

None of what is here feels beautiful anymore. It feels heavy and sad and reminiscent of a life no longer lived. I'm sorry for what I am about to do. I AM SO SORRY! Please forgive me. I need to know you're okay with this. I need a sign. Please, please show me that I have your blessing to do this. The past two weeks happened so quickly that it makes me think some other universe is pulling the strings and I'm just the puppet making the intended moves and gestures."

Sobs continued to rack my body. When the tears finally subsided, I felt strangely empty, almost cathartic but still shaken.

I continued in a more controlled voice," Mark, Mark, please know that you will always be with me. I will not let this world forget you. You're with me always wherever I go. You're not in the furniture, you're in my heart and as long as it beats, you're alive within me. I just need to go. I can no longer live in a home created for two with only one left to painfully miss the music, laughter, and sounds of our life here."

The shrill ring of the landline phone snapped me to attention. "Hello?"

"Hi, it's Jason. I know you signed the contract today and I just want you to know that I think you are doing an amazing job. I know this is a hard day for you, but Tina and I are so proud of you."

I breathed and pushed out a gentle, "Thank you," before we transitioned to mundane topics and then hung up.

Phone still in hand, I wandered into the living room. I sat at the piano where Mark so often played, and smelled it, breathing deep. There's no question. Mark's signature cologne spreads over the room as an invisible vapor. I look up and smile. *I love and miss you, my sweet man.*

Final Note

I first want to thank you for picking up this book, thumbing the pages, and deeming it worth a read. I am eternally grateful. I was handed the joy of writing from my father, who was known in our family for the poems he included in every card and the songs he wrote throughout the years. This was the best gift my father could have given me and little did I know how well it would serve me as I grappled with life's opportunities and unpredictable bends and twists.

Even though my dream as a young girl was to publish a book, I did not envision publishing this book. I found myself in the depth of despair following Mark's death and I turned to the most familiar and safest place I knew—the written word. I literally wrote my way through my grief. I didn't know this at the time, but a few years in, I felt my load begin to lighten. I began to breathe, and I saw possibilities for my life after his death. The written word began to carry my burden and the freer I became, the more I was able to write.

As we are led to discover in life, even the depths of despair can hand us a gift. In the course of my journey, I have shed much. I have sharpened my perspective of what's important to me and have tried to nurture those relationships and experiences. I finally sold my house and much of its contents. It was another exercise in grief to let go of what physically defined my life. I felt I was betraying Mark and abandoning my job to keep him alive. It was my writing that helped me understand that creating a shrine did little or nothing to keep him alive. The furniture he sat on may have evoked memories, but my heart contained every morsel it needed to keep him by my side each day. I think it was a healthy move to step away, embrace a new place to be, and live in the light he worked so hard to give me. Still, it was horrid. But I did it and am glad I did.

I believe nothing is relatable, as each loss is unique. I also believe, however, that the grieving process requires people. I know with great certainty that this book allowed some wonderful people to come into my life, both real and made up. If I hadn't taken a chance on that snowy winter day to reach out to Rebecca L. McCarthy, my talented editor and writing coach, I would have neither this book nor the treasured friendship that sustains the distance between us. Rebecca's interest in what I have to say and her encouragement that my journey would indeed give voice to what others have experienced gave me grit and allowed me to keep the pace. Rebecca, you have taught me so much about leading a writerly life, and I'm better for every conversation, every question you placed before me, every nod to take a risk, and every laugh we shared along the way. You are forever in my life and heart.

Tina and Erika are my forever champions, as I am theirs. No daughters could be loved more. You're smart, you're funny, you're kind, and you make me proud always. You chose well in Jason and Michael—I love them as the sons they are. And don't get me started on the five little peanuts! Ethan, Matthew, Mason, Zoe, and Reid—it will *always* be about you. You're what it's about for all of us.

As for friends, I've managed to collect a circle of great ones. You're all my besties because you all play such an important role in my life. Maddie, Mona, Penny, Judy, Leslie, Tina—you're the most fun people I know. And Pat, you are yet one more gift Mark gave to me and you stand alone and in front, in a special compartment of my heart.

I am not a better person without Mark—that could never be—but I do believe I have evolved into a different person who Mark would be proud of. It's his voice that tells me daily to say yes to life, to take on each new experience, to hone and polish my love for my children and grandchildren, and to honor him by leading a life he modeled for us—one of gratitude, generosity, and kindness.

I know I've written about the challenges I've faced in life. I don't think these challenges have been any more or less difficult than anyone else's. In fact, I know others have endured far worse with greater bravery and wisdom. But I hope I've also conveyed the many joys I have, the many blessings I count each day, and my gratitude for all I've been given.

I welcome you, my dear readers, into my life should you choose to walk together for a bit. If you think that sharing your story, asking questions, or just releasing what is in your heart will help you or others, please hang out with me at **robynslane.com** and **dimesonthesidewalk.com**. I would love to continue the conversation with you.

Robyn Lane is a graduate of Teachers College, Columbia University, where she earned a master's degree in school supervision and administration. She also has a master's degree in curriculum and education from Fordham University. She taught in Bedford, New York for many years before becoming an elementary school principal in Scarsdale, New York. Recently retired, when not writing she spends her time with friends and family, particularly her five adorable grandchildren and one equally cute grand-dog.

Made in the USA
Middletown, DE
20 March 2020